People of the Bible

THE WESTMINSTER PRESS PHILADELPHIA

PEOPLE OF THE BIBLE

by CECIL NORTHCOTT

designed and illustrated by
DENIS WRIGLEY

INTRODUCTION

The Bible is a panorama of living people. It is a vast gallery of portraits stretching across human life, with all kinds of people crowding into it.

All these people play their part in the Bible story which reveals God's purpose in dealing with people.

'People of the Bible', written in simple, clear language, for adults as well as juniors, brings to life the significant people who make Bible history.

The story keeps closely to the Scriptures in describing the basic events of the Old and New Testaments as they affect the people concerned in them. It offers a view of the Bible which is living and vital. It is concerned with the people God used in revealing his divine purpose seen supremely in Jesus Christ who is at the heart of this great panorama.

'People of the Bible' is a companion volume to 'Bible Encyclopedia for Children' whose illustrator, Denis Wrigley, had the skilled advice of G. H. Lankester Harding, C.B.E., F.S.A., for twenty years Director of the Department of Antiquities in Jordan.

CONTENTS

© 1967 Cecil Northcott
Library of Congress Catalog Card No. 67-12336
Printed in Great Britain
Published in the U.S.A. by
The Westminster Press ®
Philadelphia, Pennsylvania

1 MAKING OF THE PEOPLE

In the beginning God created the heavens
and the earth . . . and God created man
in his own image . . . to have dominion
over every living thing that moves upon
the earth.   *Genesis 1. 1–28.*

THE BIBLE begins its wonderful panorama of people with the Hebrew story of how
the first man and the first woman came to be. They were the first people to know
about God, for it was God who created them and their world.

Before God's spirit began to move over the vast, dark spaces of water, there was
emptiness. There was no life at all anywhere. There were no fish in the waters, no birds
in the air, no trees or flowers. There was no earth. It was a world without life of any
kind until God's spirit began to give it shape and order. His presence brooded over
everything.

With no earth to live on, there were no human beings. There never had been any.
There were no children, no families, no people.

The first act of God in this lifeless world was to create light. No living creatures
could live without light. Light was the first need of the world God was creating. So
out of the darkness God called, 'Let there be light', and he gave a name to the new
creation. He called it Day while the darkness was named Night.

As the Light spread through the great spaces it fell on water everywhere. There was
no dry land for people to walk on, no land to grow food. It was then that God divided
the waters and dry land appeared and he gave them their names—Seas and Earth.

From the earth sprang up the plants, the trees, the vegetables. From the sea came
the fishes large and small. The trees burst into leaf and then into fruit-bearing. Life
on earth began to flourish, and in the sea swam the great fishes. But there was yet no
living person.

As the earth was divided from the sea, so, above them both, God created Heaven,
and into the heavens he built the stars and with them two really great lights—the Sun

to shine by day and the Moon by night. The world as we know it began to take shape and the Bible says that at every stage of his creation God was pleased with his work.

Living creatures began to walk the dry land called earth—creatures of all kinds—cattle and beasts, insects and creeping things. They found their homes in the growing forests, on the great plains and among the mountains.

God blessed his creation of day and night, earth and sea, and of living animals and growing trees and vegetations.

THE BREATHING OF LIFE

Then God made man from the dust of the ground, said the Hebrew writers, and breathed life into him, so that he became a living being, able to walk, think, speak and make decisions for himself. Man was made superior to the fish in the sea, and to the animals on the earth. He was that part of God's creation which had a mind to use. Man had a 'soul' as well as a 'body'. He was made of 'spirit' as well as 'flesh'.

For his new creation God made a home in a well-watered 'garden'—a region of the newly created earth where great rivers ran. It was given the name of Eden, or Delight, for in it the trees seemed to flourish at their best, the fruit bushes bore their crops in great abundance, and in the warm, sunny days and cool nights man enjoyed his new home.

But God saw that man needed a companion. So, according to the Hebrew tradition, while man slept, God took one of his ribs and out of the bone of that rib God created a new human being and gave her the name of woman, and the first two people in the newly created world were named Adam and Eve.

As they lived on in the garden they wandered through its cool and shady groves enjoying its beauty and wonder. All the fruit which grew in the garden was theirs. They could pick and eat as much as they wished, but there was one tree which bore

much fruit that belonged to God alone. It was the tree called 'the tree of the know-ledge of good and evil'. Adam was not to eat of this tree for it contained the secrets of life and death which were God's secrets. But Eve was tempted to eat the luscious fruit which looked so lovely that she picked and gave some to Adam and they both ate of the tree which belonged to God alone.

'I was tempted to eat,' said Eve, 'because the Evil One whispered to me that eating the fruit would make us like God. We should then know all that God knows. We should know the difference between good and evil. We should become as wise as God.'

So Adam and Eve had to leave the Garden of Eden to live and work in the stony soil of unproductive land, where by the sweat of his brow Adam toiled to grow food for his family. They had to learn that only God could give the knowledge of life.

For Adam and Eve the lessons of life came the hard way. Their sons Cain and Abel quarrelled and Cain killed Abel, and made the deed worse by denying that he had any responsibility for his brother. 'Am I my brother's keeper?' he asked. He turned away from his family and from God and became a wanderer on the face of the earth.

Thus sin and misery came into human life and the human family, and from the hopeful beginnings of Creation, the world turned into a sad and unhappy place. But Adam and his descendants were not all cast away from God's favour. Even the murderer Cain was protected by God and many men lived in obedience to God.

The secrets of life are in God's hands—a truth which men of all times have to learn.

THE ONE JUST MAN

One man in particular 'found favour with God', and through this one man, Noah, God planned to show the world of sinful men that, though he could destroy all life, yet he could also save it.

God said to Noah that he had determined to bring his creation to an end. He would bring upon the world an immense flood which would blot out all that he had made. But Noah and his family should be saved in the ark which Noah was to build, and in

God's promise to Noah did not fail—nor to the animals two by two.

the ark, floating on the waters, the animals which God made would also be safe.

The great ark was 450 feet long, 75 feet wide and 45 feet high. It was big enough, so the Hebrew story recounts, to include all God's creation and its very size assured Noah of God's protection. Down came the rain, and the floods rose and lifted the ark above the earth as the waters engulfed all creation. Every living thing, man and beast, was drowned in the great flood except Noah, his family and animals.

After the ark had come to rest on the top of a tall mountain, Noah sent out a dove to see whether the waters had gone down. But the dove found no resting place anywhere in the vast seas of water. But the second time the dove was released she came back with a piece of green olive leaf in her mouth. Noah then knew that God had not forsaken him and that the waters were subsiding. God himself had saved Noah and had saved his own creation too.

To make this doubly plain God set in the sky the many-coloured rainbow, which in the glistening light of a rainy sky still shines with the promise of God that never again would he destroy the world because of man's sin and pride.

But men's pride kept creeping in and the ancient Hebrews used to tell the story of how men built a mighty tower—the Tower of Babel—which was to reach up to the heavens. It was to be a famous place to show what men could do. There they would speak one language and boast of the mighty achievements of men. But God shattered their ideas, compelled them to speak many languages and the tower was uncompleted.

This was the beginning of the world of people as the ancient Hebrews related it in drama, poetry and story. They saw God always present with people. It was his world even though men were disobedient and proud. God continued to be their God.

The story of the Bible's people is now ready to welcome the first great man—Abraham—who was a trustful and obedient friend of God.

Genesis 1–9.

2 ABRAHAM, FRIEND OF GOD

> The Lord said to Abram 'Go from your country, and your kindred and your father's house, to the land that I will show you. And I will make of you a great nation'. *Genesis 12. 1–2.*

THE MORNING sun sent its rays across the rows of black tents outside the city of Haran. One by one the flaps of the tents, made from the skins of animals, were raised and eager faces peeped out into the morning light. The day of departure had come. The camels tethered to their stakes, the donkeys hobbled by their legs and the goats herded in groups within their little compounds, all seemed to know that the great adventure was about to begin.

In the middle of the host of black tents stood the big one belonging to Abram and his wife Sarah. Near it was the tent of his nephew Lot and his wife. Uncle and nephew were ready to move together into a new world under the guidance of God.

Abram had been living at Haran for many years, but he was old enough to remember the time when his father Terah took all his family away from their old home at Ur, far to the south. He remembered Ur for it was a city of fine buildings and many men of culture. Lying between the two great rivers—Tigris and Euphrates—Ur used their water to irrigate the gardens and farms, and water always meant life and good living

As a boy Abram wandered into the city of Ur from his tented home outside the walls to marvel at its style and beauty and to compare it with his home of rough tents set in the windy, sandy desert. He discovered too that the men of Ur had a name for his family and people. They called them the 'Hebrews'—the ones who were always on the move, the people who moved from oasis to oasis. His friends in Ur called him 'Abram the Hebrew'. He rather liked the name. He was proud of it.

Abram remembered all these things on this bright sunny morning at Haran, as the animals were watered and the goats milked before the journey started. Terah his father was dead and he himself was seventy-five. But he was eagerly looking forward to the new journey, because he believed he was being faithful to his father's memory and obedient to the Great Spirit his father had told him about, who, he believed, would guide his footsteps.

Long before the heavy heat of the day, the caravan was on the move. The black tents had been folded on to the camels' backs and boys of the families were each given a camel to guide. Other boys saw to the goats and the donkeys as they straggled at the edges of the caravan. The total company of Abram and Lot was three hundred people, and most of them walked.

It was a steady, unhurried march. Abram was guided to swing westwards away from the great rivers into the hill country which lay south of Damascus. Every night they hoped to reach a stream, or well, to give water to the flocks of animals upon whose well-being depended Abram's wealth and the happiness of his people.

TRUST IN ABRAM

But why was he leaving the comforts of Haran? Why leave the rich grass and the streams of the land he knew for the unknown country ahead? This was the puzzle that many of Abram's people talked over as the caravan moved on. Their only answer was to trust their 'father' Abram. They were his people, and they believed that the Great Spirit—the God Abram spoke of—would lead them to a new life. They could only trust Abram.

Abram and Lot part company but still remain friends.

Abram marched on at the head of his people. Made strong and sinewy by his active life of movement under the sun and stars, Abram was also constantly aware of the Great Spirit that was leading him on. He called him 'the Lord'. He knew that the Lord

was more than wood or stone. He was more than the idols of the people he met on the way. He was the Lord of heaven and earth, the Creator of Day and Night. This was the Lord who had commanded him to go forth not knowing whither he was going.

So when Abram came to the town of Shechem in the hill country of the Canaanite people, he built an altar to the Lord, and the word came to him that this was the land that Abram and his descendants would eventually possess. Steadily going southwards, Abram followed his guidance, even as far south as Egypt where Pharaoh took notice of the wealth of the wandering stranger and gave him food and water.

But on their way back from Egypt the people of Abram and Lot began to quarrel because there was not enough water and grass for their animals. This was an age-old problem of a people on the move. How could they share the pasturage for their flocks without quarrelling? Abram and Lot finally settled the problem by agreeing to separate and to go their own ways in the new land.

'Let there be no strife between you and me,' said Abram to Lot, 'and between your herdsmen and my herdsmen: for we are kinsmen.' So Lot went off with his people and their flocks to the valley of the Jordan, while Abram turned into the hill country round Hebron and there once again built an altar to the Lord.

ABRAM'S VISION

One night as he slept in his tent in Hebron, Abram had a vision. In the vision the Lord spoke again to him.

'I will make you the father of a great people and your children shall come into great possessions and possess the land that you are now in. I will make a covenant with you, an agreement that shall last forever.'

Abram woke up and wondered about the meaning of this vision of God. How could this promise happen seeing that he and his wife Sarah had no children, and they were now both very old? Was God mocking him? He had come a long way from his old home at Haran, faithfully following the guidance of God. How was he to be the father of a great people? Abram was so troubled about this that, according to the custom of the times, Sarah gave him her serving maid, Hagar, as a wife and Hagar bore Abram a son who was named Ishmael. But still Abram was troubled in spirit that although Ishmael was his natural son yet his own wife Sarah had no son. How could his descendants be truly God's people unless he had a son by Sarah?

'Listen to me, Abram,' came the voice of God, 'no longer shall your name be Abram, but Abraham, meaning, the father of a multitude of nations. Your wife Sarah shall bear you a son.'

Abraham wondered whether this could be true.

One morning in Hebron, he was sitting in the doorway of his tent which he had pitched among the oak trees to get shade from the sun. Abraham was enjoying the cool shade of his tent when he looked up and saw three men standing among the trees. Seeing they were strangers and travellers, he immediately rose to greet them. 'Welcome,' he said, 'stay to wash your feet and to eat with us. Come into the tent.'

The strangers bowed and thanked Abraham who hurried to tell Sarah to bake bread quickly, and to kill a tender calf and roast it for the visitors. Then when the bread and the milk and the meat were ready, Abraham stood by under the oak tree while the visitors ate.

'Where is Sarah?' they asked.

'She's in the tent,' Abraham said.

Inside the tent Sarah, nervous with excitement, was eagerly listening to the conversation.

'She is to have a son,' they said.

'A son,' said Abraham, 'she's too old, and so am I too old to be a father.'

'But nothing is too strange or wonderful for God,' said the strangers. 'At this time next year Sarah will have a son.'

Inside the tent Sarah laughed out loud at the very idea that she should have a baby in her old age. It amused her greatly, but as Abraham's wife she was prepared to believe that this wonderful thing could happen to her as the visitors prophesied.

ISAAC IS BORN

In due time Sarah's baby boy was born to her and Abraham, and they named him Isaac. By the birth of the boy, Abraham's faith in God and God's faith in Abraham were finally sealed. In Isaac, Abraham saw the future hope of his people, and on the day of Isaac's weaning Abraham had a great feast to give thanks to God. God had given him a son and on that son's life the future of the Hebrew people depended. The long drama of the descendants of Abraham had begun.

Isaac grew up in the tented home of his mother and father. He early learned that the Hebrew people of his father Abraham were different from the surrounding tribes who worshipped stones and trees as their gods. Isaac noticed too that his father often

sat quietly in the doorway of their tent, looking far away into the distance as if he saw something there that no one else saw. Sometimes he went to the little stone altar among the oak trees and stood before it in silence. His father spoke often of the Lord, but to young Isaac the inner meaning of that phrase was still hidden.

One day his father called to him.

'Isaac, come with me. We are going on a journey. Get one of the donkeys ready and come with the two servants and bring a load of wood.'

The little group started off on the three-day walk to the district of Moria. Abraham was strangely silent all the way. He walked rather wearily and Isaac noticed that his father seemed sad and unhappy.

On the third day Abraham ordered the servants to take the wood off the donkey's back and put it on the shoulders of Isaac.

'Stay here,' he said to them, 'and wait for us until we come back from our sacrifice.'

'But, father, where is the sheep for the sacrifice?' asked Isaac as they walked along. 'We have the things to make the fire and I have the wood. But where is the sheep?'

'God will provide the sheep, my son,' said Abraham, 'let us have faith in him. Here is the place of sacrifice.'

Taking the wood from Isaac's shoulders Abraham piled it on the stone altar he had built. With Isaac's help he arranged it neatly on the altar and then suddenly he seized Isaac, laid him on top of the wood and bound him to it. Taking the knife from his belt,

Isaac carries the wood to the altar, but where is the sheep for the sacrifice?

13

Abraham held it aloft ready to kill his only son.

Then came a voice. 'Abraham, Abraham. Do not lay a hand on the boy. I know that you fear God since you have been ready to sacrifice your only son. Look around.' Abraham looked and there, caught by its horns in a bush, was a ram which he took and sacrificed in place of his son.

After this supreme test of faith in God, Abraham knew that in Isaac his hopes of being the father of a great people would come true. So he despatched his confidential servant Eliezer to his old home in faraway Haran.

'Go,' he said to Eliezer, 'and find Isaac a wife among the maidens in Haran, one who belongs to our own people.'

A WIFE FOR ISAAC

So Eliezer set off on the long journey back to Haran, taking ten camels and many presents of gold and silver to show how wealthy and important his master Abraham was. At the great spring of water outside Haran, Eliezer knew that he would meet many young women, some of them perhaps belonging to the families of Abraham's relations who still lived in Haran.

Eliezer made a little plan for choosing the young wife-to-be. He would stand by the well as the young women came at evening to draw water and ask one of them to give him a drink from the jar. If she offered to give water to his camels also that would be a sign that she was just the right sort of woman to be Isaac's wife.

The first young woman to come with a jar on her shoulder was very beautiful to look at.

'If you please,' he said to her, 'let me drink a little water from your jar?'

*Water in the well!
Rebecca did not forget
that the camels were
thirsty too.*

'Drink, sir,' she said, and quickly lowered the big jar from her shoulder and raised it to his lips.

'But what about your camels?' she asked. 'I will draw water for them too—all ten of them.'

To water ten camels was a long and hard job and the girl was kept busy filling the drinking trough for the thirsty animals while Eliezer watched and waited for the moment to thank her. Taking a heavy gold ring and two gold bracelets from his treasures Eliezer presented them to her.

'Tell me your name,' he said. 'Whose daughter are you? Is there room in your father's house for us to stay the night?'

'My name is Rebecca, my father is Bethuel, and I have a brother Laban. I will go to tell them,' she replied.

Dazzled with the splendour of the gifts, Rebecca hurried home with the news of her meeting at the well, and before long her brother Laban came down to invite Eliezer to come with his servants and camels to lodge at their home.

There Eliezer told the story of Abraham and Isaac and of Abraham's hope to find a wife for Isaac from people in Abraham's old home. The next day he looked again at Rebecca and saw how lovely she was, and then he said to Laban, her brother:

'Tell me, can my master have Rebecca for his son?'

'Yes,' said Laban, 'here is Rebecca; take her.'

'Wait for ten days,' pleaded Rebecca's mother.

'Let us ask Rebecca,' said Eliezer who was anxious to start on the long journey home.

'Will you go, Rebecca?'

'I will,' she said.

Then Eliezer brought out the bride's silver and gold presents, and the ones for her mother and father and brother. The camels were got ready, and with many farewells

15

to her family, Rebecca and her maid mounted their camels and followed Eliezer and his men on the long journey to her husband and her new home.

When she first met Isaac, according to the custom of the time, she covered her face with her veil. But when she was alone with him she lifted it and Isaac saw for the first time the beauty of the young woman who had come to be his wife, and from that time onwards he loved her dearly.

Genesis 12, 13, 17, 18, 22, 24.

3 JACOB, FATHER OF ISRAEL

He dreamed that there was a ladder set up on the earth, and the top of it reached to heaven...the Lord stood above it and said, '...the land on which you lie I will give to you and to your descendants...and by you and your descendants shall all the families of the earth bless themselves'.

Genesis 28. 12-14

TO ISAAC and Rebecca were born twin sons, Esau and Jacob. They lived with their parents in the land of Canaan, shepherding the flocks and herds, and tilling the farm lands of their father. Esau was a hunter, an expert with the arrow and the bow. He loved the open-air life and his ruddy face and hairy hands showed how much he lived out on the hills hunting for game. Jacob, a quieter man, happy to be the shepherd of his father's sheep, was the favourite of his mother Rebecca.

One day Esau came in from hunting very hungry, and he burst into the tent where Jacob was cooking some food. It smelt good and Esau was greedy.

'Give me some of that food, Jacob,' he said, 'I'm so hungry I'll give you anything you want for it.'

'All right, sell me your birthright then,' replied Jacob.

'Yes, even my birthright. I'll swear you shall have it. It's not much good to me.'

For the sake of a little stew of bread and lentils, Esau gave away his most precious heritage—the birthright of a first-born son. The crafty Jacob had won first place in the family, and hoped to get Isaac's fatherly blessing too.

Over the hills went Esau.

Jacob's bowl of savoury meat for his old father.

THE BLESSING FOR JACOB

When Isaac was old and his sight was failing, Rebecca planned to get the old man's blessing for her favourite son. One day Isaac said to Esau that he would dearly love to eat a savoury meal of meat and would then bless Esau before he died. So Esau went off to the hills to hunt the game. Rebecca saw that this was her chance.

'Go to the flock,' said Rebecca to Jacob, 'and bring two choice kids and I will make a savoury meal for your father. Cover your hands with hairy skins, so that when your father comes back he will think you are Esau. Quick, before Esau comes back.'

Jacob did as he was told and went into his father's house, carrying the food.

'Here I am, father. I am Esau, your son. Here is the food. Give me your blessing.'

'Come near, my son,' said the old man, 'so that I may be sure that it really is Esau. Your voice is surely the voice of Jacob, but your hands are the hands of Esau.'

The deceitful trick worked and Isaac gave Jacob his blessing which established him as Isaac's heir and as the father of the Hebrew people.

Soon afterwards Esau came in from the hills and, when he realized what had happened, was ready to kill his brother. Jacob had taken his birthright and now he had taken his blessing. The two brothers separated in bitter hatred.

From that bad beginning of deceit and trickery, Jacob had to make a new start, and the first need was to find a wife from his mother's people in Haran. So Jacob set out for Haran, with the blessing of Isaac, to choose a wife from the daughters of his uncle Laban.

Just outside Beersheba, as he tramped on to Haran, Jacob made a resting place for the night. There on the ground he used a stone as a pillow to sleep out in the warm night under the stars. Tired out with the day's walk, he soon went to sleep and dreamed that he saw a ladder reaching from earth to heaven with angels running up and down on it. The voice which had spoken to his grandfather Abraham spoke to him, and Jacob heard the words:

'I am the Lord, the God of Abraham and the God of Isaac. I will be with you and protect you wherever you go. I will not forsake you.'

17

Then Jacob rose from his sleep and said, 'Truly the Lord is in this place. This is none other than the house of God; this is the gate of heaven.' He poured oil over the stone, and set it up as a memorial, and made a vow that if he made a safe return to his father's house he would build an altar on the spot.

Rachel came with her sheep and captured Jacob's heart.

JACOB'S TURNING-POINT

Jacob's dream was a turning-point in his life. From then on he knew that the promise of friendship made between God and his grandfather, Abraham, was coming true for him. Jacob became a new kind of Jacob, more kindly and more humble.

He walked on into the lands of the east until he came to the country round Haran and found the family of his uncle Laban. The first to greet him was his cousin Rachel. She came to the well to water her sheep and there for the first time Jacob looked at the beauty of his wife-to-be. Her grace and dignity, as she shepherded her sheep towards the well, captured Jacob's heart. He watched her standing in the sunlight among the sheep, and as she came nearer her beautiful dark eyes fascinated him.

Usually the shepherds waited for all the flocks to be assembled round the well before they rolled back the big stone which guarded its mouth. But Jacob, eager to show affection to Rachel, at once rolled back the stone himself and watered her sheep.

'I am Jacob,' he said to her, 'the son of Rebecca, your father's sister.'
At the news Rachel ran to her father's house and Laban came to greet Jacob.

That was the beginning of Jacob's long years of service to Laban in return for Rachel as his wife. For fourteen years he served Laban faithfully as shepherd and manager of his affairs. Laban's flocks and herds grew in numbers, for Jacob proved himself a good workman.

'I believe God has blessed me because of you. Stay with me,' said Laban, 'name your wages and I will pay.'

'Give me nothing,' said Jacob, 'but let me choose the speckled goats and black lambs. They shall be my wages.'

So the bargain was struck between the two men. But secretly Jacob departed with his family, the speckled goats and black lambs, and set off on the long journey homeward to the land of Canaan.

Jacob contrasted his homeward journey with the lonely one he had made years before. Now he was rich in cattle, and flocks and herds, and had many children. God had blessed him, and Jacob knew that his future happiness and that of his family depended on his faithfulness to the guidance of his God, the God of Abraham and his father Isaac.

But disturbing news reached him from his scouts, ahead of the main party. They reported that Esau was on the march towards him. Esau! The brother who hated him, the brother whom he had deceived, the man who had been ready to kill him.

So Jacob planned a wonderful offering of friendship and peace for Esau. He chose from his great herds some of his finest animals and sent them in separate processions to Esau. First 200 she-goats, then 20 he-goats, followed by 200 ewes, 20 rams, 30 milch camels with their young, 40 cows, 10 bullocks, 20 she-asses and foals. Esau was astonished at the sight of such generous gifts, and they softened his heart towards his brother.

As the last procession moved towards Esau, Jacob followed and bowed himself to the ground seven times until he reached his brother. Esau ran to Jacob, and the two men wept and embraced each other, and became friends again.

Jacob woke to the beauty of the dawn. God had given him a new name.

JACOB'S NEW NAME

Jacob journeyed on towards the city of Shechem, and one evening as the light began to fade, he sent all his people across the River Jabbok, which flows into the Jordan, while he remained alone on the other side. There God appeared to him and wrestled with him. That was how it seemed to Jacob, as all night he debated with God.

'Let me go,' came the Voice, 'it is nearly dawn.'

Jacob refused to let go.

'I will not let you go,' he said, 'unless you bless me. Tell me your name. Tell me your name,' pleaded Jacob, 'are you God?'

'Why do you ask my name?' came the answer. 'I will give you a new name as a sign that you have been with God. From now you shall be called Israel.'

As the first light of dawn came, Jacob lay exhausted on the river bank. He had seen God, and had been given a new name. Jacob himself became a new man. God had spoken to him and placed his hand upon his life.

So Jacob and his people passed on into the land of Canaan, and, at Bethel, Jacob built an altar to the Lord and ordered his people to purify themselves, to rid themselves of strange idols, and to remember they were people of the Lord.

As if to crown his happiness, Rachel gave birth to another son—Benjamin, the last of his sons and next to Joseph his favourite boy. But his birth cost Rachel her life, and she was buried near Rama to the north of Jerusalem where Jacob marked her grave with a memorial.

With her Jacob buried the memories of his life. He was now Israel, the Father of a people, and with them was about to take another mighty move under the guidance of God.

Genesis 25. 29–34, 27–35.

So proud of his coat.

4 PEOPLE OF THE AGES

And God spoke to Israel in visions of the night, and said, 'Jacob, Jacob.' And he said, 'Here am I.' Then he said, 'I am God, the God of your father; do not be afraid to go down to Egypt; for I will there make of you a great nation. I will go down with you to Egypt, and I will also bring you up again; and Joseph's hand shall close your eyes.'
Genesis 46. 2–4

JACOB LOVED Joseph most of all his sons. He was the son of Rachel, and in Jacob's old age Joseph was a reminder to the old man of his early devotion to Rachel, and of the long years he spent in wooing her. He pampered Joseph. He gave him smart clothes to wear, including a very special coloured coat with long sleeves, which Joseph loved to show off to his brothers.

Joseph was in many ways a spoilt boy and he showed off by telling his family of the dreams he had. In one dream he said they were all gathering sheaves in the harvest field, when suddenly his sheaf stood upright and those of his brothers bowed down to it. In another dream, he said the sun, moon, and eleven stars worshipped him. What did this mean? wondered his father. Did it mean that Joseph was destined to be

a great man and a great ruler? The old man wondered deeply about the dream. But Joseph's brothers began to hate the young dreamer.

One day when the brothers were far away in the hills of Shechem pasturing their sheep, Jacob decided to send Joseph to see that all was well with them.

'Go,' said Jacob, 'give my greetings to your brothers and come back and report to me.'

After much wandering over the high country, Joseph found his brothers at Dothan. They saw him coming, and plotted against him.

'Here comes the dreamer,' they said. 'Let us take our chance to get rid of him. Let us throw him into a pit and say that a wild beast has killed him.'

But Reuben protested at the idea of shedding blood. 'Throw him into the pit but don't kill him.' So Joseph was thrown into a deep pit which was empty and dry. Soon after that the brothers saw a caravan of merchants with their camels carrying gum, balm and myrrh, on their way down to Egypt.

'Let us sell Joseph to these merchants,' said Judah. 'Let us save his life by sending him away.'

JOSEPH SOLD INTO EGYPT

For twenty pieces of silver Joseph was sold to slavery in Egypt, and his brothers went home to their father with his coat of many colours dipped in the blood of a goat.

'Look, father, we have found this coat. Is it Joseph's coat?' Jacob recognized the coat and saw the animal's blood, and believed the story of his deceitful sons that Joseph had been killed by a wild beast. With many tears and much sorrow, Jacob mourned for his lost son and refused to be comforted.

Down in Egypt, Joseph was bought by Potiphar, one of King Pharaoh's chief officers. Potiphar liked the young man and soon made him chief manager of all his affairs, giving him authority over his household, his property and his money. Joseph grew

'Let us sell Joseph to these traders,' said his brothers.

up a handsome and attractive young man, and so attractive was he to Potiphar's wife, that she planned to make him her lover, but Joseph refused, and Potiphar's wife had him arrested and thrown into prison.

In the prison of Potiphar's house Joseph met the royal butler and the royal baker, who were also out of favour and had been imprisoned. The two men confided in Joseph that in their sleep they had vivid dreams. Could Joseph explain them? So well did Joseph interpret these dreams that when the butler was released and was reinstated in the royal service, he told Pharaoh about Joseph, and Pharaoh sent for him.

'I dreamed,' said Pharaoh, 'that I was standing by the bank of the River Nile and I saw seven cows, fat and sleek, feeding in the rich grass. Then seven other cows came along, ugly, lean and scrawny, and these cows ate up the seven fat cows. Then in my dream I also saw seven fine ears of grain growing on a single stalk. Then seven withered ears of grain sprouted and swallowed up the seven fine ears. What do you make of the dream?'

'God is speaking through this dream,' said Joseph to Pharaoh. 'There will be seven years of plenty and then seven years of famine. You now have time to prepare for the seven years. Collect all the food you can, and get ready for the lean years.'

Pharaoh, the king, made Joseph one of his chief men.

So Pharaoh appointed Joseph to carry out his seven-year plan. All over Egypt the granaries and barns were stacked with grain. In the cities the people were trained to store and conserve food, and in the villages every acre of land was tilled and cultivated.

Joseph's plan worked splendidly. He rode in his own chariot dressed in handsome robes with a gold chain about his neck, and all through Egypt Joseph's name was known and respected. When the years of famine came, Egypt was ready to face them.

The famine extended all through the lands of the East, and even into Canaan where the land failed to provide food enough for Jacob's family.

'There is food in Egypt,' Jacob said to his sons. 'Go down there and buy for us that we may live and not die.'

So ten of Jacob's sons went down to Egypt and interviewed Joseph, who instantly recognized his brothers.

'You have come as spies,' he said. 'You have come to spy out the weak spots of the land.'

'No,' they said. 'We are the sons of Jacob in the land of Canaan. Our youngest brother is at home with our father. We have come to buy food. Here is the money.'

'If you are honest,' said Joseph, 'go back to your father and bring your youngest brother to see me, and let one of you stay here as a sign of good faith.'

The silver cup! The silver cup! It's found in Benjamin's sack.

BENJAMIN ARRIVES

So Simeon stayed behind in Joseph's prison, while the brothers went home to tell their father of this strange man in Egypt who seemed to know all about them. Joseph had filled their sacks with grain and even put back the purchase money in the sacks.

The news terrified Jacob. Here was someone in Egypt who had uncanny powers. Who was this man? He had lost Joseph, and now they wanted to take Benjamin. In sorrow and distress the old man let Benjamin go to Egypt, never expecting to see him again.

This time Joseph received the brothers more kindly. When he saw young Benjamin, his brother, he wept.

'Is your father living?' he asked. 'Is he well?'

He sat them round the table, gave them food from his own plates, and feasted them richly—always giving Benjamin five times more than the others.

'Fill up their sacks with grain,' Joseph ordered, 'and put my silver cup in the sack of Benjamin.' So the brothers set off for home, happily satisfied to have got food and to have brought Benjamin out of Egypt safely.

They had not gone far, however, before messengers from Joseph caught them up.

'Our master's silver cup is missing. Have you stolen it? If it is in one of your sacks then the owner must return and be imprisoned.'

The terrified brothers, frightened at the news, hunted through the sacks and to their horror found Joseph's cup in Benjamin's sack. They turned back to Joseph's house and fell down in terror at his feet.

'Do not send us back to our father without Benjamin,' Judah pleaded. 'Our father is old and the boy is everything to him. He will die if Benjamin does not return. Take me in his place as your slave.'

At last Joseph could control himself no longer. He burst into tears before his brothers and confessed, 'I am Joseph your brother whom you sold into Egypt. Do not be terrified at what you did. God sent me here before you to prepare the way, to save your lives and the life of my father and of Benjamin.'

23

'Bring my father Jacob. Tell him there is food here for all his people.'

JACOB IN EGYPT

The frightened men knelt before him, unable to speak. They gazed in silence at the man who had only love in his heart for his brothers.

'Go quickly to my father Jacob,' said Joseph, 'and tell him that Joseph is alive and well in Egypt. Bring him down into Egypt and I will prepare the land of Goshen for you to live in. There are five years of famine yet to come. But there is grain and food here, and in Egypt, Jacob and his people will be happy.'

The brothers hastened back to their father Jacob with the good news. Joseph loaded them with presents of silver and clothes, and much grain and provisions, and he warned them not to waste time quarrelling on the way, but to bring Jacob and the people from Canaan before Jacob was too old.

So Jacob came into Egypt with his goods and cattle, his herds and flocks, his children and grandchildren, and settled in the land of Goshen under Joseph's protection. He divided among them the choicest portion of land, provided a plentiful supply of grain in the famine years and gave to them in brotherly love an example of how the Hebrew people should live together.

Jacob died in extreme old age and, faithful to his promise, Joseph carried his body back to Hebron in the land of Canaan, and buried it in the field that had once been his grandfather Abraham's. It was a sign that one day the Israelites would return from Egypt to the land of Canaan.

Genesis 37–47, 49

24

5 PEOPLE OF THE GREAT JOURNEY

I have seen the affliction of my people who are in Egypt, and have heard their cry because of their taskmasters; I know their sufferings, and I have come down to deliver them out of the hand of the Egyptians, and to bring them up out of that land to a good and broad land, a land flowing with milk and honey.... Come, I will send you to Pharaoh that you may bring forth my people, the sons of Israel, out of Egypt. *Exodus 3. 7–10.*

THE HOT sun beat down upon the dry and stony soil and sent a shimmering haze of heat as far as the eye could see. The short, scrubby bushes offered very little for the sheep to eat, and Moses, the shepherd, had to keep his eyes open for the shady places where the grass was less parched. The sheep belonged to Jethro, his wife's father, and in the long, hot days of his shepherding, Moses had much time to think.

As he walked with his sheep in this wilderness of Horeb, Moses was thinking about himself and his future. Why had he come to this wild and lonely country? Why was he a shepherd in this scrubby, desert land? What had the future in store for him?

Suddenly, in the bright hot sunshine, he saw ahead of him a flame of fire. It leaped up in the heart of a bush. The flames seemed to envelop the whole bush, but to his amazement the bush was not destroyed. The flames burnt on and as he walked a voice spoke within the flames.

'Moses, Moses, do not come too near; take off your shoes, walk in your bare feet, for the place you stand on is holy ground.'

Covering his face with his hands so that he could not see the flames, Moses heard again the voice speaking.

'I am the God of your father, the God of Abraham and Isaac and Jacob. I have heard the cry of my people in Egypt, and the time has come for them to leave Egypt and you are to be their leader.'

'But who am I,' said Moses, 'to lead my people out of Egypt? Who am I to go to Pharaoh and to demand that the people be freed? No one will listen to me. I am not eloquent. I am only a shepherd of these sheep in the wilderness.'

'I will be with you,' said the voice. 'I am the God of your fathers. I am Yahweh, and I will lead my people into the land flowing with milk and honey. Listen to my voice and obey it. Go back into Egypt, and prepare my people.'

Standing there in front of the flaming bush Moses knew that God was speaking to him. In the stillness of the desert he felt the presence of God, and the burning bush made God more than ever real to him. Slowly he turned away from the bush.

25

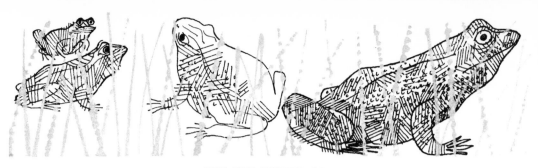

Frogs, frogs, frogs, they covered the land.

LET THE PEOPLE GO

He knew that the time had come for the Hebrew people to move out of Egypt. For years they had lived in misery under the Pharaohs, who used them as menial slaves to build their cities, and even compelled them to make their own bricks of clay. Gone were the days of Joseph when the Hebrews were a favoured people in Egypt. Gone were the days of plenty of grain for baking bread in the land of Goshen. The Hebrew people were now hated by the Egyptians and many Hebrew babies had been killed in infancy. Moses himself had escaped from one of those massacres by being rescued from the bulrushes of the River Nile where his mother had hidden him in a little cradle. There Pharaoh's daughter found him and adopted him into her household, with his own mother as his nurse. She never let him forget that, although living as an Egyptian, yet at heart he was a Hebrew. As a young man he had even killed an Egyptian whom he saw torturing a Hebrew, and to escape with his life he had to flee into the desert and become a shepherd.

All these things Moses remembered as he went back into Egypt at God's command to ask Pharaoh to give the Hebrews their freedom.

'Who is this God you speak of?' asked Pharaoh. 'I do not know him. I will not let Israel go. They are an idle lot. They must work harder. They must now make their bricks with no straw to help them.'

So under the lash of Pharaoh's slave-drivers' whips the life of the Hebrews got worse and worse.

Nothing that Moses and Aaron could do softened the heart of Pharaoh who, while he hated the Hebrews, also wanted to keep them in Egypt as slaves. But God prepared the way for the deliverance.

Moses smote the waters of the Nile with his rod and the river turned into blood, and all the fish died and no one could drink the water. Seven days later he caused a plague of frogs to cover the land, and then followed plagues of gnats and flies, of boils and hail and locusts. The people of Israel saw the power of God in all these plagues but Pharaoh's heart was still hardened towards them. At last came the terrible night when all the first-born children in Egyptian homes died and a great cry of sorrow rose from Pharaoh and his people.

It was on this night that God warned Moses and Aaron to tell their people that each Hebrew family should kill a lamb, and sprinkle its blood on the door-posts of their

26

house. This was the sign of the 'passover'. Every house showing the sign was 'passed over' and saved from destruction—a deliverance that the people of Israel remembered ever afterwards in the Passover Meal.

'Go,' said Pharaoh to Moses, 'take your flocks and herds and be gone.'

So Moses and Aaron led the people out of the land of Goshen towards the Sea of Reeds on the first stage of their journey back to the land of their fathers in Canaan, and as they marched a pillar of cloud went before them in the clear sky and at night a pillar of fire as signs of God's guidance.

But the great exodus had hardly begun before Pharaoh repented of what he had done, and gathering a great host of chariots and horsemen he pursued the Israelites to the Sea of Reeds. There he planned to catch them. But a strong east wind blew across the Sea as the Israelites arrived on the shore and drove back the waters so that they were able to get across on dry ground. But when Pharaoh's men came to cross, the sea rushed in again and the great Egyptian host was drowned.

FOOD AND WATER IN THE DESERT

As Moses stretched his hands over the sea in thanksgiving he and the people sang a song of thanksgiving. How many people there were no one knows exactly. Long weary miles lay ahead of them through the dreaded wilderness of Sinai.

Moses knew that water would be their chief problem. He had learned a good deal about desert life from Jethro, his father-in-law, so when the water at Marah tasted bitter, and the people complained, he threw into it the bark of trees, which seemed to make it sweeter. At Elim, the oasis of palm trees and twelve springs of water made a beautiful camping ground, but as they marched on into the wilderness so water and food got scarcer.

Down to the sea went chariots and horsemen.

'Give us bread,' cried the people. 'In Egypt we had plenty to eat. But you have brought us here to kill us all by hunger.'

Then Moses taught the people to look around for food, to use what God was providing for them. In the evening flocks of quail settled on the ground and were easily captured. In the morning a sticky, sugary substance formed on the low bushes like little peas. When it dried in the sun it was good to eat and the people called it 'manna'. But Moses warned them not to gather manna on the seventh day for that was the 'Sabbath', a solemn day of rest and worship of God. Step by step across the wilderness the people learned to be dependent on God, to watch the cloud by day and the fire by night as signs of God's presence, and to be obedient to God's instructions.

When they came to the oasis at Rephidim the place was dry and the people were thirsty, but striking the rocks with his rod Moses made the spring of water flow again. Then a wild desert people, the Amalekites, descended on them to stop their march.

For a whole day the battle went on, with Moses' hands lifted up to encourage the Israelites. Whenever he let them fall the Israelites lost ground, so Aaron sat Moses on a stone and held up his hands until the battle was won.

AT MOUNT SINAI

As they moved nearer Mount Sinai Moses began to prepare himself and the people to meet God. The great mountain was wrapped in thick cloud, with lightning flashing through the mist and the long roll of thunder echoing round the top.

'I am coming to you in a thick cloud,' said the voice of God to Moses, 'that the people may hear when I speak. Obey my voice, keep my covenant, and you shall be a holy nation.'

So the people washed their clothes and stood at the foot of the mountain while Moses climbed to the top and entered into the presence of God. The whole mountain quaked in thunder and out of the smoke came the sound of trumpets while the first of the great commandments was given to Moses, 'I am the Lord your God . . . you shall have no other gods before me.'

'Speak for us,' said the people to Moses. 'We are afraid.'

'Do not fear,' said Moses. 'God has come to you that you may obey him and become his people.'

But while Moses was away on the mountain, the people grew impatient and disobedient.

'Let us make gods for ourselves now,' they said to Aaron. 'Moses is a long time on the mountain. We may never see him again. We want gods to worship.'

So collecting their gold rings they melted them down and made a golden calf, and worshipped it with dancing and singing.

But when Moses came down from the mountain he angrily threw the calf into the fire and ground it to pieces.

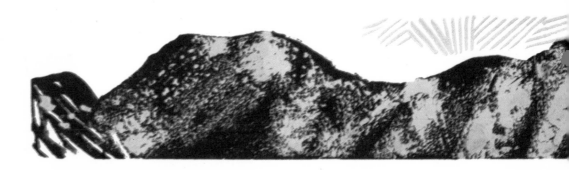

'You have sinned a great sin,' he cried 'and I must go to the mountain again and ask God's forgiveness for what you have done. There is no other God.'

So Moses moved once more into the thick cloud of the mountain and heard the voice of God telling him that between God and the people of Israel a compact was made and that for all time God would care for Israel and be their God. To make this clear to all the people, Moses built an altar at the foot of Mount Sinai and offered a sacrifice on it, and read aloud to the people the laws of God he had received, and they all answered in a loud voice, 'All that the Lord has spoken we will do, and we will be obedient.'

To remind the people constantly of God's presence as they marched on through the wilderness, Moses built a large oblong tent, or tabernacle, divided by curtains, which could be carried as they marched. To contain the commandments he had received from God, he built an ark of acacia wood kept in the inner 'holy of holies' of the tent.

Moses on Mount Sinai heard the voice of God.

This simple, movable temple was a sign of the presence of God and the beginning of Israel's 'temple worship'. To care for this 'tent of meeting' and the worship of the people, Moses appointed Aaron and his sons as priests.

Moses knew that they could not stay for ever at Mount Sinai. The long road to the Promised Land still lay in front of them. But instead of an unorganized horde of marchers, Moses now led a people who knew that they were moving under the orders of God. The Sinai experience welded them together as one company.

So, carrying the 'tent of meeting' and the scrolls of the law, the people of Israel moved on to the borders of the Promised Land. They still grumbled about the lack of food and water, endured plagues of snakes, and fought with desert tribesmen. But the hopes of the people now were here on the land they had heard about and dreamed of.

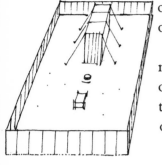

The sacred 'tent' in the desert.

THE PROMISED LAND

To find out more about this land, Moses sent out twelve spies, one from each tribe, including Joshua, the future leader of the people.

'Go up into the country ahead,' he said, 'and see what the land is like, what sort of people live there, and whether the cities are strong or weak.'

The spies came back with a divided report. They all agreed the land was wonderful and that it flowed with 'milk and honey', but ten of them were frightened by the power and might of the fierce tribes who were ready to fight all invaders. They had no chance against them. But Joshua and Caleb urged Moses to march at once while the people of Israel were still strong. God would be with them.

But under the pleading of the people Moses gave way and directed them to turn southwards in order to come into the Promised Land through what is now the land of Jordan. It added many weary miles of desert to their pilgrimages, with many battles against desert tribes who fought hard to prevent the newcomers reaching their new home. During these years of wandering the Israelites grumbled at Moses and often turned away from the worship of the one true God. Moses again and again brought *Promised Land over the Jordan.* them back to be loyal to the God who was leading them. He gave them careful instructions in ways of worship and exact duties for their daily conduct, and, above all, he appointed Joshua as a new leader of the people.

Moses was growing old. The long years of desert life had tired him out, and as he drew near to the River Jordan, and the border of the Promised Land, he knew that he would never enter it. There in the land of Moab he stood on the high point of Mount Nebo and looked out over the land. It was a wonderful sight. He could see the trailing curve of the River Jordan as it cut its way down the deep valley and emptied itself in the Dead Sea. Far to the north he could just see the shape of another stretch of water which Israel was to know later as the Lake of Galilee, and beyond that the high mountains of Mount Hermon with their tops in perpetual snow.

Just across the border from where Moses stood to view the land was Jericho, with its vineyards and fig trees, its lush grass and water—a city worth capturing, but one which Moses was never to enter. All this looked wonderful to him. For years he had lived the hard life of the desert, but in all the worst moments of this desert journey his dream of the Promised Land kept his hope alive. It was this hope that kept his people alive too, and now Moses knew that the dream of the desert was going to come true.

As he stood there, shading his eyes with his hand and looking out over the landscape, Moses also knew that it was more than the hope of a new home that had brought him and the people to this spot. In the desert, God had been making them into his own people. From being separate groups of wanderers they had been shaped into a 'people'. In the years of hard life in the desert, Israel had become an instrument for God to use. And Moses had been God's chosen man in the great enterprise.

LOOKING INTO THE FUTURE

As he strained his eyes towards the distant horizon of the Promised Land, Moses also thought of the future of his people. He had brought them out of Egypt, through the perils of the desert, to this turning-point in their history. Now they had got to cross the River Jordan and capture the first of the cities of their new land—the city of Jericho —the first task of Joshua's leadership.

But as the old man stood on Mount Nebo, thinking of the past and dreaming of the future, he could see beyond Jericho. His old eyes looked into the far future when Israel would be happily settled in their new home and would be truly the 'people of God' both in worship and conduct. Would God then speak to them again? Would he show himself ever more wonderfully to them? Moses wondered.

So Moses came down from the mount of vision, content to pass on his leadership to the younger man—Joshua. He died in his great old age of one hundred and twenty, and while the people of Israel mourned for him for thirty days they also sang a song of thanksgiving to God for Moses who had led them to the Promised Land.

Exodus 3–40; *Numbers* 13–14; *Deuteronomy* 32

Moses saw the Promised Land but never entered it.

31

'Up on the roof,'
said Rahab, 'you
will be safe.'

6 PEOPLE IN THE PROMISED LAND

As I was with Moses, so I will be with you; I will not fail you or forsake you. Be strong and of good courage; for you shall cause this people to inherit the land which I swore to their fathers to give them.   *Joshua 1. 5–6.*

'QUICKLY, UP to the roof,' said Rahab. 'They have come to search for you.'
Rushing up to the flat roof the two spies of Israel lay down and Rahab covered them with the stalks of flax she was drying in the sun. Looking down into the street she saw the messengers from the King of Jericho at her doorway.

'The men are not here,' she said. 'They came before the gates of the city were shut but they've gone. Go after them quickly as far as the Jordan.'

Running back to the spies lying on the roof Rahab told them the way was clear for them to escape. But first of all she made them promise that when Joshua and the people of Israel captured Jericho they would save her and all her family.

'Our life is yours,' said the men. 'If you do not give us away we will see that your life is spared. Put a scarlet cord in your window so that the besiegers will know to save your house.'

Then Rahab let the men down over the wall of Jericho and they escaped to Joshua with the news that Jericho was a frightened city and that now was the moment to attack. Now was the hour for Israel to advance.

So Joshua ordered the people to begin the march across Jordon. They followed the Ark of the Covenant which contained the commandments given to Moses by God on Mount Sinai. Step by step, the priests bearing the Ark, together with twelve men from the twelve tribes, came to the River Jordan. Slowly and carefully the priests went down to the water's edge, dipped their feet into the river, and led the people safely to the other side.

After years of journeying and hoping, they were now in the land of Canaan. There could be no turning back now. Joshua began to prepare himself and his people for the attack on Jericho.

One day, as Joshua was making his plans for the attack on Jericho, he met a man carrying a drawn sword in his hand.

'Are you for us, or against us?' Joshua asked.

'I am commander of the army of the Lord,' was the reply.

Then Joshua realized that, like Moses, he was seeing a vision of God.

'Take off your shoes,' said the man, 'for the place you stand on is holy.'

Suddenly the vision ended and Joshua knew that he was to attack immediately.

Joshua ordered his army to march round and round the walls to frighten the fearful people cowering inside the city, and to encourage his own men too. Some blew on trumpets and made a great noise by shouting in order to impress the Jericho men with the strength of the Israelite army. For six days they marched and trumpeted and on the seventh day the whole host of the people appeared before Jericho, and in a mighty, surging shout, the crumbling walls of Jericho shook, and where breaches were made the Israelites rushed into the city, burning and killing as they went. Only Rahab and her family were saved.

JOSHUA THE CONQUEROR

Then Joshua moved on towards Ai. Encouraged by what had happened at Jericho he sent only three thousand of the people to capture the city. But the men of Ai came out of their city and put up a brave fight and chased the Israelites away.

On hearing the bad news Joshua fell on his face, tore his clothes, and put dust on his head. He knew that someone among the people must have disobeyed his orders. Someone must have stolen silver and gold in Jericho which he ordered that no one should touch because it all belonged to God.

The men of Ai left their city gates wide open. Joshua's men rushed in.

33

Every tribe in Israel was carefully examined and suspicion fell on Achan and his family. Achan admitted that in Jericho he had stolen shekels of silver, and a beautiful mantle. It was all found hidden in the earth inside Achan's tent. Then Achan and his family and all his cattle and sheep were put to death by stoning and burning. It was a terrible punishment, but Joshua believed that the Israelites would never conquer the land unless they obeyed God's commandments to the very letter. Achan was a stern example the Israelites never forgot.

Joshua captured Ai by a clever ruse. He divided his army into two. One section was hidden in an ambush near the city while the other section attacked the city and pretended they were defeated. They ran away as the men of Ai repulsed their attack and so drew out the Ai men from their city. They left the gates wide open and pursued the fleeing Israelites, and then Joshua's other army rose and entered the city and set it on fire. So when the men of Ai looked back they saw their homes burning behind them, and hardly any of them escaped alive.

TRUST NOT IN ARMIES

Now the Israelites began to spread out through all the hill country, conquering local kings and cities as they went. With headquarters at Bethel and Shechem Joshua established the Israelite power, although he did not conquer the whole of the country, and never captured Jerusalem. Like his great master Moses, Joshua was continually reminding his people that their true greatness lay in their worship of Yahweh—the Lord their God. They were not to depend on the might of their arms but on becoming a people dedicated to God.

How difficult all this was, Joshua knew only too well. After the years of journeying in the desert, and the struggle to win a place for themselves in the land of Canaan, the Israelites wanted to have an easier time. Many of them were tired and wanted to settle down to farming and vine growing. They wanted to enjoy this land of 'milk and honey'. They got interested, too, in the way the Canaanite people worshipped, for the Canaanites had gods who, they said, governed the weather, speeded the growth of crops, gave young to their animals and helped human beings to have children.

Religion among the Canaanites seemed very exciting, with lively festivals for the gods. How different it was from the stern, unseen God the Israelites had been taught to worship, whose laws were so strict. No wonder the Israelites 'ran after other gods'.

A land of 'milk and honey'. How wonderful after life in the desert.

The chariots of Sisera.

THE NEW LEADERS

With no great leader to follow Joshua, the people of Israel went after other gods, and forgot whose people they were. They disobeyed the commandments given to them on Mount Sinai, and followed the customs of the Canaanite tribes. Then God raised up a group of local leaders called 'judges' who tried to keep the people true to their faith.

One of them was Deborah, who lived in the northern hill country, where Jabin, the King of Hazor, was fighting against the Israelites. Jabin had a powerful general called Sisera, whose very name struck fear into Barak, the Israelite leader.

'If you will go with me,' said Barak to Deborah, 'I will go to the battle.'

'Surely I will go with you,' said Deborah. 'Gather the army to fight Sisera. But I prophesy that this time God will deliver Israel through the hand of a woman.'

So ten thousand Israelites faced the nine hundred chariots of Sisera near Mount Tabor, and under the inspiring leadership of Deborah gained a great victory. Even Sisera, the feared general, was forced to leave his chariot and flee on foot. As he fled, Sisera came to the tent of Jael, wife of Heber the Kenite, who invited him in to rest. As the Kenites were friendly towards Sisera's people, the general, tired out with the battle, felt safe and lay down in the tent where Jael gave him milk to drink and covered him up to sleep. As he slept Jael saw her chance to kill Sisera and to rid Israel of its enemy. Creeping up to him, Jael hammered the sharp end of a tent peg into Sisera's forehead.

So Deborah's prophecy came true and the people of Israel celebrated the victory with a wonderful poem of thanksgiving.

After Deborah, Gideon, the farmer, arose to lead the people in the ways of God and to defend themselves against the raids of the Midianites who stole their grain and cattle.

As Gideon threshed his wheat secretly in the wine-press instead of in the open field for fear of the Midianites, a voice spoke to him:

'The Lord is with you, Gideon, you mighty man of valour.'

'But, if this is true, why are we in this miserable condition at the mercy of the Midianites? Where are the great days our fathers told us about when God delivered us from Egypt?' asked Gideon.

'You are to be the deliverer now, you, Gideon.'

Gideon threshed his wheat in secret.

35

'But I belong to the smallest of all our families. Who am I to be a leader?' said Gideon.

'I will be with you, and you shall smite the Midianites as one man.'

To make sure that God was calling him, Gideon made a test. He put out a fleece of wool on the threshing floor, and said, 'If God wishes me to be leader, let there be dew on that fleece, and none on the ground.'

In the morning Gideon found the fleece wringing wet and the ground dry.

So Gideon sent out a call to the people to rally to his leadership, and they came in thousands to fight against the Midianites. There were so many that Gideon devised a plan to reduce the number. He marched the men to a stream to drink. Thousands of them drank the water greedily, putting their faces right into the stream. But three hundred men were more alert and scooped up the water with their hands. With these three hundred men Gideon marched to the fight with trumpets blowing and torches blazing, and the frightened and half-awake Midianites fled in disorder.

Gideon was now Israel's hero, but even he and his son Abimelech, who established himself as a local king, failed to give Israel the leadership which was acceptable to all the people.

All around them the Midianites, the Ammonites, the Moabites and the Philistines, constantly raided and fought them. To resist the Philistines there rose up a powerful judge-prophet, called Samson, a member of the strict Nazarite sect. He never cut his hair, believing that his great strength lay in his long hair. He used to taunt the Philistines and even killed some of them using only the jaw-bone of a donkey. Then he was betrayed by his woman friend, Delilah, who cut his hair. Helpless, Samson was at last captured, blinded and imprisoned by the Philistines. Samson, the mighty Israelite, became a laughing-stock of the Philistines, but he had his revenge. The Philistines brought him out of prison one day to give a display of his strength at a feast. In one mighty heave Samson wrecked the pillars of the palace where the feast was going on and so killed the Philistine leaders and himself.

But the time had come for a new leader to arise.

Hannah brought Samuel to serve in the Temple.

SAMUEL THE KING-MAKER

In the temple at Shiloh, Eli, the old priest, conducted the worship as best he could with the aid of his two worthless sons. One day there came to the temple a young mother, called Hannah, with her only son Samuel. She wished him to serve the Lord as a young assistant to Eli, and the old man, growing old and blind, took the boy to help him. It was not long before Eli realized that Samuel was an unusually intelligent and devoted boy.

One night as Samuel slept in his place in the temple, he heard someone calling him,

'Samuel, Samuel.' Thinking it was Eli, he ran to the old man, only to be sent back to bed again. At the third time Eli realized that the boy was hearing the voice of God.

As Samuel opened the doors of the temple next morning he was afraid to tell Eli what God had told him about the wrong-doing of his sons. But Eli insisted that he should know and Samuel told him the honest truth.

From that time on, news about Eli's young assistant began to spread through Israel, and he grew to be respected by the people as a prophet in Israel.

Samuel travelled round the country, visiting the people at the chief places of worship. He was partly judge, partly military commander. It was Samuel who encouraged the Israelites in all their fights and raids with the Philistines. He organized groups of prophets to go around among the people to remind them of the promises they had made to God, and of what God expected of them. Samuel ruled Israel almost like a king—except in name. He was the greatest of the 'judges' and was the forerunner of the 'prophets' who came later in Israel's life.

Samuel realized that the time had come for him to pass on his authority to a new type of leader, when he heard the people asking for a 'king' to rule them, someone who would be their monarch in fact as well as in name. To seek for a man worthy to become king became the chief task of Samuel as he grew into old age.

Joshua 1-12; *Judges* 4-8, 13-16; 1 *Samuel* 1-8

7 PEOPLE AND KINGS

Long live the King!
God save the King!

> 'We will have a king over us, that we also may be like all the nations, and that our king may govern us and go out before us and fight our battles' . . . And the Lord said to Samuel, 'Hearken to their voice, and make them a king.'
> *1 Samuel 8. 19–22.*

ALL THE people shouted, 'God save the King.' There he stood, head and shoulders above everyone else—a handsome young man, looking the part of a leader, ready to be king over the people of Israel. Samuel anointed him with oil, and presented him to the people. His name was Saul, a young farmer of the tribe of Benjamin.

'Long live the king,' shouted the people.

But both Samuel and Saul knew that this eagerness to have a king was a fickle phase on the part of the people. They wanted to be like all the other surrounding tribes and forgot their special place as the people of God who was their only king.

Some people said, 'How can this man Saul save us and lead us?' They despised him. But others rallied to the standard of Saul, who began his reign with a call to Israel to

37

save the besieged city of Jabesh, whose people were threatened with destruction. Following Saul, the people marched to the relief of Jabesh, and Saul's right to be a victorious leader was established. All Israel acknowledged him.

Saul was helped by his gallant and popular son, Jonathan, celebrated for his single-handed exploits against the Philistines. At the hill fort of Michmash, Jonathan, with one armour-bearer, climbed up the outside of the fort, crept over the top, and their sudden appearance so frightened the garrison that they all fled in a panic. His exploits thrilled the people and when Jonathan ate some honey on a fast day and so endangered his life by breaking his oath to fast, the people demanded that he should not die. 'As the Lord lives,' they said, 'there shall not one hair of his head fall to the ground.'

THE COMING OF DAVID

But Samuel, the old prophet, longed to find someone who would lead Israel more strictly in the ways of God, and at last he was led to the family of Jesse, the Bethlehemite.

'Find a king among Jesse's sons,' was the divine message to Samuel. But when Samuel came down to Jesse's home he found seven sons to choose from. They were all brought before him, he admired them all and thought that almost any one of them would make a king.

'Are all your sons here?' Samuel asked Jesse.

'There is one more,' said Jesse. 'He is out keeping the sheep. I'll send for him.'

The boy David, the youngest of the sons, came in, his face shining with youth and health. God said to Samuel,

'Arise, anoint him, for this is he.'

So there in his father's farmyard David was secretly anointed to be, some day, leader and king over Israel, and champion in the fight against Israel's enemies.

His fight with the giant Philistine Goliath was the most celebrated of all his youthful exploits.

Goliath terrified the Israelites. They had no one like him and no one who could fight this man equipped with such armour and such a sword. One day when Goliath was swaggering and boasting before the army of Saul, David had come to the camp with food for his brothers from their father. He saw how crestfallen the Israelites were.

'Let me fight Goliath,' said David to his brothers. They all laughed at the idea. But the news spread to Saul that a young warrior had arrived in camp ready to fight the Philistine giant. Eager to snatch at any help, Saul dressed David in a suit of armour with a bronze helmet and a coat of mail.

'No,' said David. 'I cannot wear these. Let me take my sling and a few stones. I have killed lions and bears with them.'

Goliath roared with laughter at the sight of a mere boy with a sling. But as the giant came towards him, David saw a place in the giant's forehead unprotected by his helmet. Taking a sure aim with his sling, he sent a smooth stone to the vulnerable spot and Goliath fell, and David ran and using Goliath's own sword cut off the giant's head.

David then became a favourite with Saul, who loved to hear him play on the harp for the music soothed his bad temper. Jonathan, Saul's son, also loved David and gave him many presents of fine clothes and armour. David married Saul's daughter, Michal, and the future for him seemed happy and prosperous.

But when the people began to celebrate David's fame and exploits against the Philistines in preference to those of Saul, the king's affection turned to jealousy, and from jealousy to hatred, and from hatred to enmity.

Just a boy—with a sling, a smooth stone, and faith in God.

'Take care,' said Jonathan to David, 'my father seeks to kill you. Stay in a secret place and hide yourself.'

So David lived in the wild open country between Bethlehem and the Dead Sea in caves and on the hills. Like a hunted man he was often in danger of his life, often hungry and homeless with Saul's trained warriors always on the alert to capture and kill him.

On one occasion David himself crept into Saul's tent and could have killed the king while he was asleep, but he merely cut off a piece of Saul's robe and sent it to the king with the message, 'I will not put forth my hand against the king; for he is the Lord's anointed.'

But at last Saul himself was defeated and killed in battle with the Philistines, and with him also died David's friend, Jonathan, for whom David sang a beautiful lament:

> I am distressed for you, my brother Jonathan;
> very pleasant have you been to me;
> your love to me was wonderful,
> passing the love of women.
> How are the mighty fallen.

2 Samuel I. 26–27

Solomon and his temple were wonders of the world—even the Queen of Sheba came to visit.

KING IN JERUSALEM

The way was now open for David to become king of all Israel. To make this real for all the people, David established his rule in Jerusalem, and brought the Ark of the Covenant into the city so that all Israel could see that the Lord God was at the heart of the kingdom. He reorganized the army, defeated the Philistines, built himself a palace in Jerusalem and ruled wisely and well. One of David's most thoughtful acts was to invite Mephibosheth, the crippled son of his friend Jonathan, to make his home in the palace, a friendship which won the hearts of his enemies who still looked back to the days of Saul.

But for all his wise rule David had many weak points in his character. He could be covetous, greedy and selfish. One of his worst acts was his marriage to Bathsheba, the wife of one of his best soldiers, Uriah the Hittite. In order to get rid of Uriah, David had him sent into the front of a battle against the Ammonites, and there he was killed. But David's treachery became known to Nathan the prophet, who denounced him to his face, and David deeply repented of his cruel selfishness. The first child born to David and Bathsheba died, but their second son lived to become king after his father. He was given the name of Solomon.

David too was unhappy in his relations with his favourite son, Absalom, who plotted against his father and tried to become king in his place. Handsome and popular with the people, Absalom reminded David of his own youthful days, and his heart went out to his rebellious son.

'Deal gently for my sake with the young man Absalom,' he ordered his soldiers in battle. But it was Absalom's pride that killed him. Riding through the forest, his long beautiful hair caught in the branches of an oak and left him hanging, to be speared to death by his pursuers.

David's reign ended in a mixture of sadness and glory. For forty years he had given the people of Israel a firm and secure rule. He had tried to govern according to the laws of God, and to be true to the covenant between God and Israel. His last words to his son Solomon charged him 'to be strong and show yourself a man, to keep the charge of the Lord your God, walking in his ways and keeping his commandments'.

SOLOMON'S TEMPLE

To show his loyalty to this great trust, Solomon set to work to build a permanent temple for the worship of Yahweh ('the Lord') in Jerusalem. Never before had the people of Israel had a fixed house of the Lord. In their wanderings the tent of the tabernacle had been carried from place to place. Now, with the kingdom established, Solomon's Temple was built in great grandeur. It was 90 feet long, 30 feet wide, and 45 feet high, in stone and rich cedar wood overlaid inside with gold. It had two rooms —the Holy Place and the Holy of Holies, where the two cherubim, or winged lions, representing the presence of God, glistened in gold.

In the outer court of the Temple two pillars, 27 feet high, stood upright on the porch, which itself was 30 feet high. In this courtyard was a gigantic basin containing 10,000 gallons of water, supported by 12 oxen representing the 12 tribes of Israel. Here too were 16 golden candlesticks, the table of the holy shewbread (representing the food God had provided in the wilderness) and the great altar for sacrifices.

It took seven years to build this great house of God, and Solomon enriched it further with magnificent bronze ornaments, with flowers, lamps, cups, basins and dishes carved in gold, so that the whole Temple became an expensive wonder for all Israel. The people slaved to build and paid heavily in taxes for the cost. The Temple glorified God. But it glorified Solomon too.

SOLOMON'S FAME AND WISDOM

Solomon's fame spread through all the world. Even in Africa the glory and wisdom of King Solomon attracted the attention of the Queen of Sheba. She collected a great caravan of camels and attendants, and with a huge present of spices, gold and precious stones arrived in Jerusalem to visit Solomon.

'I heard reports of your wonderful city,' she said, 'and also of your wisdom, but I did not believe it all until I came to see and hear for myself. But only half the story was told me. What I have seen is far more wonderful than I had imagined.'

Solomon's ships too brought treasures to Jerusalem.

There were many stories of Solomon's wisdom. On one occasion two women came to him carrying a baby. These two women lived in the same house and about the same time both gave birth to babies. But one baby died in the night, and secretly its mother stole the living baby and placed the dead one by the side of the other mother. Each woman said the living baby was hers. To which mother did the baby really belong? The two women quarrelled and at last came to King Solomon to solve their quarrel.

The king said, 'Bring me a sword, and divide the living child in two, and give half to each woman.'

'No, my lord,' cried one mother. 'Do not kill the baby. Give the living baby to the other woman. Let her keep it.'

But the other woman said to the king, 'Divide it. The baby shall not be mine or hers.'

Then Solomon gave judgment that the first woman to speak was surely the true mother of the baby because she cared above all that the baby should live.

All Israel praised this wisdom of Solomon and praised him even more at the great feast which he made for the dedication of the Temple, when thousands of sheep and oxen were sacrificed. There, with arms outstretched, Solomon stood to bless all the assembly of Israel and prayed, 'The Lord our God be with us, as he was with our fathers; may he not leave us or forsake us; that he may incline our hearts to him, to walk in all his ways, and to keep his commandments which he commanded our fathers.'

Israel was proud of her king, who had made Israel's name famous throughout the world. Solomon's ships sailed the seas. Solomon's wisdom, and Solomon's sayings were on men's lips everywhere. Solomon 'in all his glory' had made the throne of Israel a really royal throne.

But as Solomon's reign came to an end Israel began to realize that God was leading them towards a new understanding of his purpose. He had spoken to them through the patriarchs, Abraham, Isaac and Jacob, through the wise leaders, Joseph, Moses and Joshua, through the judges, Gideon and Samuel, and through the kings, Saul, David and Solomon.

But now new leaders were rising up—the prophets. A fresh company of men was beginning to speak in the name of God to Israel, and the long process of training Israel to be 'the people of God' had reached another turning point.

1 Samuel 9–31; 2 Samuel 1–21; 1 Kings 1–11

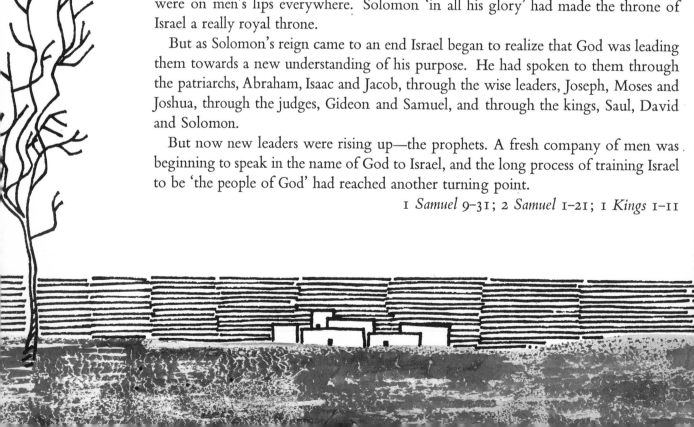

8 PEOPLE AND PROPHETS

I hate, I despise your feasts,
and I take no delight in your solemn assemblies.
Even though you offer me your burnt offerings and cereal offerings,
I will not accept them,
and the peace offerings of your fatted beasts
I will not look upon.
Take away from me the noise of your songs;
to the melody of your harps I will not listen.
But let justice roll down like waters,
and righteousness like an ever-flowing stream.   *Amos 5. 21–24.*

THE LAND was parched and dry. There had been no rain for months. Even the brooks had run dry, and Elijah the prophet, roaming over the countryside, was hungry and thirsty. Coming near a village, he met a woman gathering sticks.

Elijah called to her, 'Bring me a morsel of bread, for I am hungry.'

'I have nothing baked,' she said, 'only a handful of meal and a little drop of oil, and I am gathering a few sticks to make a fire. My little son and I will eat and then die.'

'Fear not,' said Elijah, 'your jar of meal will not be emptied and your oil will not give out. Make me a little cake.'

For days the woman and her family ate together with Elijah and the food never gave out; and when the little boy of the house fell ill Elijah revived him and gave him back to his mother.

'See, your son lives.'

'Now I know that you are a man of God, and that the word of the Lord in your mouth is truth,' she said.

ELIJAH ON CARMEL

But King Ahab thought differently about Elijah. He called him 'the troubler of Israel' because he reminded the king that he and his wife Jezebel had forsaken the commandments of God and gone after the local gods—the 'baals'—and their prophets.

'Just a few sticks to make a fire before we die of hunger.'

Elijah challenged these prophets to a contest on the top of Mount Carmel before a great host of the people.

'Let us sacrifice two bulls,' he said, 'and call on the name of our God to send fire for the sacrifice.'

All day long the prophets of 'baal' prayed to their god, and pleaded with him to send down fire. But nothing happened. Then Elijah called the people to him and prayed to the 'God of Abraham, Isaac and Jacob' to send fire on his sacrifice, and down came the fire.

The fire fell down from heaven crackling the wood, licking up the water in the trench and sending up great clouds of smoke. As the fire blazed and gradually enveloped the whole altar the vast crowd of people chanted:

'The Lord, he is God, the Lord, he is God.'

Elijah's God had won a great victory over the false gods of Ahab and their priests fled before the anger of Elijah and many of them perished in the River Kishon.

When King Ahab told his wife Jezebel all that Elijah had done she stormed in anger, and threatened to kill the prophet.

But Elijah disappeared into the wilderness and hid himself under a broom tree, hoping that no one would find him. All his fine courage was gone and he lay down wishing to die.

In his sleep an angel touched him and roused him up,

'Look, rise and eat.'

Elijah looked round and there at his head was a little cake, warm from the baking on the hot stones, and by it stood a jar of water. Elijah's courage revived, and he knew that God was still with him.

Elijah too gave up hope and lay down to die.

THE VOICE OF THE PROPHETS

The people, and their king, were fickle, and untrustworthy. Now that the kingdom was divided—north and south, between Israel and Judah—there was no strong king like David or Solomon at the centre. But the voice of the prophets reminded the people of their duty to God.

All over the northern country Elijah urged opposition against the 'local gods', and was thoroughly hated by Ahab for his straightforward, honest speech. He was followed by Elisha, whose fame as a man of God and worker of miracles spread even beyond the boundaries of Israel.

One man who heard of Elisha's power was Naaman, the commander of the Syrian army. He suffered from leprosy and came to Elisha to beg him to cure him. He came with expensive presents of gold and silver, but Elisha told him to do a very simple thing in order to be cured.

'Go and wash yourself seven times in the River Jordan,' said Elisha.

'But why in the Jordan?' asked Naaman. 'Are not the rivers of Damascus better than all the waters of Israel? Could I not wash in them and be made well?'

Naaman turned away from Elisha in anger, but his servants persuaded him to do the humble, simple act at the prophet's command. So Naaman dipped himself seven times in the Jordan and was cured of his leprosy.

Elisha's power made Israel greatly feared by the surrounding nations. The King of Syria even plotted to kidnap him. He sent horses and chariots in a raid over the border and surrounded the town of Dothan where Elisha lived.

'Alas, my master,' said Elisha's young servant, 'what shall we do? We are surrounded by the King of Syria's soldiers.'

'Look again,' said Elisha, 'look again, and you will see what God is doing.'

The young man looked and in his vision he saw Elisha protected by horsemen and chariots of fire.

The prophets spoke for God and they spoke honestly and fearlessly. After Elisha, came Amos from the remote country village of Tekoa in the south. He was a herdsman, a forester and a shepherd too, and in the deep quietness of his country life God spoke to Amos about truth, honesty and righteousness.

'You know all the tricks of the trade,' said Amos—'except truth and honesty.'

Amos went up to Bethel and spoke his mind to the people.

'You trample upon the needy,' said Amos, 'and bring the poor of the land to a miserable end. You ask when it is a good time to sell the grain in order to make a quick profit, and you play tricks with the weights and measures. You give cheap prices for good things, and sell off the poor stuff at high prices.'

This honest talk from a countryman was too much for the city dwellers in Bethel.

'Get away back to your own country,' said Amaziah the priest to Amos. 'Get your living there and not here in the city. This is the capital where the Temple is and where the king lives. We are doing everything that is right, and the king does not wish to see you, or hear you.'

Then another prophet, Hosea, rose up to speak to Israel. Hosea's wife, Gomer, had been unfaithful to him, but Hosea loved his wife and refused to be permanently separated from her, and eventually she came back to him. Hosea used this experience to make plain to Israel how much God loved her and that his love would never fail.

45

Isaiah in his vision saw the whole earth filled with the glory of God.

But a greater prophet than either Amos or Hosea arose in the land of Judah in the year that King Uzziah died, about seven hundred and fifty years before Christ was born. His name was Isaiah and he lived through the reigns of four kings—Uzziah, Jotham, Ahaz and Hezekiah.

In the year that King Uzziah died Isaiah had a wonderful vision of God calling him to his ministry.

'I saw the Lord,' he said, 'sitting upon his throne, high and lifted up. He seemed to fill all the Temple. Winged figures stood above him, ready to fly. They covered their faces and their feet in the presence of God, and flew through the Temple crying, 'Holy, holy, holy is the Lord of hosts; the whole earth is full of his glory.'

Isaiah was more than a prophet coming up from the country to accuse the city people of their wrong-doings. He himself was an educated man who looked beyond the passing events of the day to the countries surrounding Israel and Judah. He saw these two small countries gradually falling under the domination of the great power of Assyria which lay to the north. God, he said, was surely using Assyria to teach Israel that he was not only the God of Israel but the God of the whole world. Isaiah looked out on the whole world and believed that it was God's world and that everything that happened in it was related to God.

But Isaiah also lifted the eyes of the whole people beyond their present problems. Israel and Judah might be overwhelmed by the mighty armies of the Assyrians but she would still be the people of God. The hope of Israel, he said, lay, not in power and military might, not in wealth and in kings, but in the hope of being the true servant of God. Isaiah pointed the people towards the coming of the Holy One of God—the Messiah—who would bring in the reign of peace and happiness they all longed for, and he spoke it in these wonderful words:

> For to us a child is born,
>   to us a son is given;
> and the government will be upon his shoulder,
>   and his name will be called
> 'Wonderful Counselor, Mighty God,
>   Everlasting Father, Prince of Peace.'

Isaiah 9. 6

A younger prophet called Micah also joined Isaiah in preaching the truth about God's relationship with Israel and together they warned the people of what would happen to them. In the northern kingdom the Assyrian armies swarmed through the country of Samaria, and large groups of people were taken off to captivity. Once more the Israelites were homeless in a strange land and had to learn all over again the hard lessons of obedience, justice and righteousness. The people and their kings, so the prophets said, had refused to be God's people, and what was happening to them was the penalty of their disobedience.

Isaiah saw the Assyrian armies as God's judgment on Israel.

But there was a happy note too in the voice of the prophets. God, they said, would condemn, judge and punish, but he would also forgive. He would not always destroy. There would always be a few of the faithful—a little group whom God would not forget and for their sake he would forgive the wrong-doing of many. Isaiah looked forward to the time to come when there would be peace on earth for all the peoples. He sang of the time when the whole earth would be full of the glory of God and his poem describes how even the wild animals would then be shepherded by a little child, and no harm would come to the child, a time when the whole world would be under the rule of God.

The wolf shall dwell with the lamb,
  and the leopard shall lie down with the kid,
and the calf and the lion and the fatling together,
  and a little child shall lead them.

Isaiah 11. 6

They shall not hurt or destroy
  in all my holy mountain;
for the earth shall be full of the knowledge of the Lord
  as the waters cover the sea.

Isaiah 11. 9

1 Kings 17–19; *2 Kings* 5–6; *Amos* 7; *Hosea* 1–4; *Isaiah* 6–11

9 PROPHETS AND KINGS

Then the king sent, and all the elders of Judah and Jerusalem were gathered to him. And the king went up to the house of the Lord, and with him all the men of Judah and all the inhabitants of Jerusalem, and the priests and the prophets, all the people, both small and great; and he read in their hearing all the words of the book of the covenant which had been found in the house of the Lord. And the king stood by the pillar and made a covenant before the Lord, to walk after the Lord and to keep his commandments and his testimonies and his statutes, with all his heart and all his soul, to perform the words of this covenant that were written in this book; and all the people joined in the covenant.
2 Kings 23. 1–3.

ALL THE streets of Jerusalem were thronged with people hurrying to the Temple. They were eager and excited at the news they had heard. Most of them were city

48

dwellers but, through the gates, groups of countrymen were crowding in to share the excitement.

The command of King Josiah to come up to the Temple was a very special order. For the Temple had been repaired, and much money had been spent on the job. Large collections had been made among the people who had given generously to the reconstruction, and no expense had been spared. The carpenters, builders and masons had been well paid.

The excitement of the people was caused by the news that in the rebuilding of the Temple a great discovery had been made. Hidden in the Temple, the builders had found some ancient scrolls which turned out to be part of the laws and instructions given by God to Moses as the people of Israel crossed the desert. This book of laws we know as the Book of Deuteronomy.

Parts of the book had already been read to the king by Hilkiah the high priest and Shaphan the king's secretary. King Josiah, a young man of twenty-six in the year 622 B.C., was greatly moved as he heard the words of the law recalling him and his people to the ways of God. The words came over the centuries ringing in the king's ears like a great bell of truth, and the king was eager that all the people should hear too.

So the approaches to the Temple were crowded with people jostling to get into the outer court of the Temple, where the king was standing with the priests and his advisers. The outer court was packed with people and as the king, standing by one of the great pillars, took the book of laws and began to read from it silence fell over the listeners.

King Josiah ordered the people to listen to the words of the law.

THE KING READS THE LAW

Every word the king read went home to the hearts of the people as they realized how disobedient they were to the commandments of God. They could see, even in the Temple courtyard, the altars of other gods, and everyone from the country knew of the 'baal' worship that went on in the towns and villages of Judah. There were 'high places' or altars all over the country with priests who made much profit out of the pagan worship.

The young King Josiah read the great words of the law book, and he pledged himself to keep the 'words of the covenant' and all the people joined him in the pledge.

Then began a great reform of religious observances throughout the land. Many of the pagan altars were demolished, the mediums and witches belonging to 'baal' worship put away, and its idols destroyed. Led by the king the people observed the religious customs as set out in the book of laws, and all over Judah there was a return to the worship of Yahweh—the one true God.

But reform of outward observances is not enough. There was one man in the land who saw beyond this splendid attempt of King Josiah to reform the customs of the people. His name was Jeremiah, a young prophet who early began to speak in God's name. Like Isaiah he was sure that God had called him to prophesy. Like Isaiah his lips were touched and he came into Jerusalem with the stern message that only a complete return in repentance could save Judah.

JEREMIAH AND THE POTTER

Jeremiah saw the surrounding nations of Assyria, Egypt and Babylon as instruments of God's purposes. He predicted that these powerful nations would come to take the people of Israel captive. There would be famine and drought, crops would fail, the water cisterns would be empty, and plagues would bring death to many.

One day Jeremiah went to the potter's house in Jerusalem and watched him making his pots. He saw him working the clay with his hands on his wheel as it turned, and turned, gradually shaping a pot. Sometimes the clay broke in his hands as the wheel turned, and then the potter used the clay again and re-worked it into another pot.

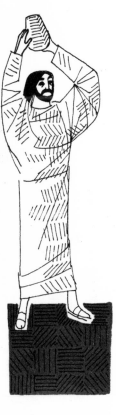

He hurled the pot to the ground and smashed it to pieces.

'O, house of Israel,' cried Jeremiah, 'can I not do with you as this potter has done?' Jeremiah stood at the city gates to preach his message, where his tall, gaunt figure drew the crowds. Many of his listeners mocked and laughed at him, and even Jeremiah himself wondered whether he was doing any good. 'Everyone mocks me,' he cried to God, 'I have become a laughing-stock all the day.'

To make his message even more dramatic Jeremiah bought a pot from the potter and went down to the valley just outside one of the city gates. There in the presence of the elders of the people and the senior priests, Jeremiah held the pot over his head.

'This is what God will do,' he said, 'this is what he will do. This city of Jerusalem will be destroyed. It will become a horrible place. Like this potter's vessel it will be broken in pieces.'

Then Jeremiah hurled the pot to the ground and smashed it to pieces in the sight of the people and the priests. All this was too much for Pashhur the chief priest. These gloomy words of Jeremiah were ridiculous, he said, Jerusalem was prosperous and happy. The chief priest saw no signs of the misery that Jeremiah spoke about. So Pashhur arrested Jeremiah, beat him, and put him in the stocks for the people to laugh and jeer at.

But that experience made Jeremiah speak all the more boldly. He prophesied that all Judah would fall into the hands of the King of Babylon, and that many of her citizens would be killed, and all the wealth and treasures of the kings of Judah would be carried off as well as many of her people.

50

Again and again Jeremiah spoke bravely as God led him to speak. He even stood in the court of the Temple and called on the priests to repent of their evil ways and to lead the people in repentance. This time the priests were so angry with Jeremiah that they stirred up the people to demand his death and got the king to confirm the sentence. Then Jeremiah stood before the assembly of priests, people and king, and said, 'Amend your ways and your doings, and obey the voice of the Lord your God. I am in your hands. Do with me as seems good and right to you. But if you put me to death, you will bring innocent blood upon yourselves and upon this city and its inhabitants, for I speak the truth in God's name.'

This fearless speaking won respect for Jeremiah. The wisest of the priests knew that what Jeremiah was saying was true, for the tides of war were relentlessly sweeping round Judah and Jerusalem. The great King Nebuchadnezzar of Babylon besieged the city and carried off King Jehoiakim into captivity, together with his mother and all the palace officials, as well as ten thousand people, with all the skilled craftsmen. Only the poorest people remained—and Jeremiah remained too to share the misery and suffering of Jerusalem.

SURRENDER OF JERUSALEM

Nebuchadnezzar's soldiers made a hole in the walls of Jerusalem, and rushed into the city.

There was worse still to come during the reign of King Zedekiah, who ruled in Judah under the overlordship of Nebuchadnezzar. The king rebelled against Nebuchadnezzar and for two years Jerusalem was besieged. Zedekiah very gallantly resisted

51

the onslaught of Nebuchadnezzar's men and fought against great odds. Jeremiah was inside the city and all the time prophesied to the king that the city would fall to the besiegers. 'Do not deceive yourselves.' he said, 'God is using Nebuchadnezzar for his own purposes. Jerusalem must surrender and her people be led into captivity.'

'Beat Jeremiah and put him in prison.'

This was such doleful and depressing news that the army leaders arrested Jeremiah for spreading the spirit of defeat. He was beaten and imprisoned in a dungeon cell and was there for many days. Then King Zedekiah sent for Jeremiah and asked him whether there was any special message for him from God.

'Yes,' said Jeremiah, 'you will be delivered into the hands of the King of Babylon.'

It was depressing news for the king, but he respected Jeremiah, released him from prison and saw that he was given a ration of bread every day. But the army leaders soon pounced on the prophet again.

'This man is weakening the hands of the soldiers,' they said. 'He is spreading the fear of defeat. Throw him into a cistern.' There in the deep, oozy mud of a waterless cistern, Jeremiah began to sink and would have died of suffocation or hunger, had not the king heard of it and sent three men to rescue him.

'Can you give me some good news, Jeremiah?' the king asked. 'Hide nothing from me.' Again Jeremiah could only advise the king that the best thing he could do was to surrender to Nebuchadnezzar for he was bound to be defeated in the end. It was God's will that Jerusalem should be conquered and her people pass through years of suffering.

But Zedekiah persisted in his hopeless defence of the city until at last Nebuchadnezzar's army made a hole in the city wall and poured into Jerusalem. Zedekiah and his sons fled but they were captured. Zedekiah was tortured by seeing his two sons killed before his eyes and was then himself blinded and carried off to lifelong imprisonment in Babylon.

JEREMIAH REMAINS IN THE CITY

The worst of Jeremiah's fears had come true, but he himself remained in Jerusalem and saw the destruction of the Temple by Nebuchadnezzar's soldiers. He saw them carry off the bronze and gold ornaments, the basins, the pots, the lampstands, the incense dishes and all the priestly vessels. All the glory of Solomon's Temple was destroyed, and hundreds of people were marched off to captivity in Babylon to join their countrymen already in exile.

Nothing now remained of the outward wonder of the Temple worship. Israel had to learn that God was not confined to the Temple and its ritual. Her God was a God who wished not for sacrifices and burnt offerings but for truth in the heart and in the actions. Jerusalem was destroyed but God lived with his people wherever they were. He would not forsake them. Jeremiah lived on in Jerusalem for a while wondering what all this suffering meant, and trying to discover what lessons God was teaching his people through these tragic experiences.

2 Kings 23; Jeremiah 7, 18, 26, 37–39, 52

10 PEOPLE OF THE GREAT HOPE

Behold my servant, whom I uphold,
my chosen, in whom my soul delights;
I have put my spirit upon him,
he will bring forth justice to the nations.
He will not cry or lift up his voice,
or make it heard in the street;
a bruised reed he will not break,
and a dimly burning wick he will not quench;
he will faithfully bring forth justice.
He will not fail or be discouraged
till he has established justice in the earth;
and the coastlands wait for his law.

Isaiah 42. 1–4.

IN THE hot desert land of Babylon, the little companies of Hebrew people began to live their life in exile in small villages. They had tramped the thousand dusty miles from Jerusalem to Babylon as captives of Nebuchadnezzar, and had seen the cruel treatment meted out to their king and his sons. They too went in fear of their lives. Torn from their comfortable homes in Jerusalem, they found life hard in the land between the two rivers—Tigris and Euphrates. Although they were not prisoners in a prison they were homeless, unhappy and longed for their own homeland.

A lovely land—but a lonely, unhappy one for the exiles.

*No music from the
lyre.*

Sometimes in despair, and always in sad longing for their old homes, the exiles sang plaintive songs, many of which are preserved in the Bible in the Psalms. This is one of them:

> By the waters of Babylon,
>   there we sat down and wept,
>   when we remembered Zion.
> On the willows there
>   we hung up our lyres.   *Psalm* 137. 1–2

They treasured their old traditions and customs and many hoped that one day they would return again to build up Jerusalem and to restore the Temple. But as the years went on the Hebrews in Babylon grew accustomed to the country they lived in. Children were born there who had never known any other home, and old people died far away from their native land. Many of the Hebrews also conformed to the habits and customs of the Babylonians, and some of them forsook the worship of Yahweh, the one true God.

Many of the Hebrews wondered why it was all this misfortune had fallen on them. Why did not God prevent it? Why did he permit them to be carried off into captivity? He must be a dead God and not a living one. His Temple in Jerusalem was destroyed, and he had no place now where he could be worshipped. The gods of other nations seemed to be far more powerful. Why should they try to keep faithful to a God who was not faithful to them?

PROPHETS OF HOPE

So argued the Israelites in Babylon. To meet these arguments and to put fresh purpose and renewed hope into the people, two prophets arose. One was Ezekiel, and the other Isaiah, whose prophecy is in chapters 40 to 66 in the Book of Isaiah.

'The Lord set me down in the midst of a valley which was full of bones,' said Ezekiel.

'Can these bones live?' asked God. 'Speak to this wilderness of dry, dead bones, and tell them to hear the word of God.'

Can dead bones live again? wondered Ezekiel, and in his vision he looked out over the valley which as far as he could see was full of bones. It was a frightening sight. All Ezekiel could see was a world of dead things which had been dead for so long that there was no chance of their living again.

But as Ezekiel stood looking, he felt a wind passing over the valley of the bones and they began to stir. The bones moved under the power of the wind. Some stood up-

'Even dry bones can live,' said Ezekiel. 'The river of life will flow through the wilderness.'

right, and others came together like a great crowd of people rushing to see and hear something wonderful.

The valley of dead bones became alive and Ezekiel saw that this was God's way of telling him that even the people of Israel, dead though they were, could live again, and Ezekiel began to move among the exiles crying:

'O my people, I will open your graves, and cause you to come up out of your graves, and bring you into the land of Israel, and you shall know that I am the Lord, and you shall live in your own land.'

EZEKIEL'S VISIONS

In another of Ezekiel's prophecies he saw a great stream of water coming from under the threshold of a house, and a man led him into the water to try to cross it. At first the water came to his ankles, then to his knees and then to his waist, and at last Ezekiel knew that this was a deep stream which could not be easily passed over. It was the holy river of God coming from under the Temple itself and flowing through the wilderness between Jerusalem and the Dead Sea. There were trees on its banks, fish in its waters and even the salty Dead Sea itself was transformed.

All this God could do with Israel. The river of new life could flow through the barren lands of her life and bring new hope and new faith.

Ezekiel spoke of his visions as he moved about the villages of the exiled Hebrews, and as they listened to this young prophet their hopes revived again. Through his pictorial visions they understood his message. Dead bones could live again! The river of water could be the river of new life! These pictorial visions spoke powerfully to the people.

Ezekiel crowned his prophecy by describing his vision of the Temple of God with its gates facing north, south, east and west. It was a striking and powerful call to the people to turn their hearts once more to God, for God would build the city and make it a holy place for all Israel.

But there was something even more wonderful for Israel to learn in exile than to hope of returning some day to Jerusalem. There was something greater that God was planning for Israel than the rebuilding of the Temple. It was the preparation of Israel to see that her God was the God of all the world, of all nations, and all peoples.

'Don't you know,' asked Isaiah, 'that the God you worship is the God of all creation? He stretches out the heavens like a curtain, so that the sky is like a vast tent for people to live in. From where God sits above the world we are all like grasshoppers.'

Isaiah's vision helped the lonely and sad people of Israel to see that their God was no local god like the gods of Babylon. He was the creator of the universe whose power would last for ever. If they returned to him he would forgive them and save them.

He alone was God. He could create, judge and condemn. He had dealt sternly with Israel when she rebelled and fell away from her faith. But he was gradually training Israel to understand her place in the world. He was her judge but he was also her redeemer. Isaiah began to speak words of comfort to the people which inspired them to believe that their sins would be forgiven. His poem of comfort gave hope to all the people.

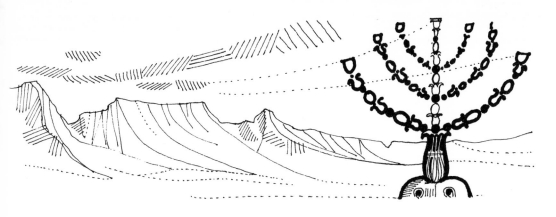

Israel was to be a light to all the world.

ISRAEL AS SERVANT OF ALL

'The day of exile is drawing to an end,' said Isaiah, 'and the day of redemption and hope is coming near.'

Even while they were still in the land of exile, in the land of suffering and sadness, there was something new for Israel to learn.

Isaiah's vision for Israel was that among the nations of the world she should show herself as one who was ready to suffer and to serve. He saw the people of Israel as having a very special mission to all the world—to teach mankind how to live.

Israel was to be the 'servant of God', the people who were ready to be humble, meek, gentle, forgiving, and ready to give their life for others. This was the new note which Isaiah sounded in the ears of the people. It was a strange note to some and they did not understand it. They all knew what suffering meant, but how could they also be asked to bear the sins of others and to forgive those who did them wrong? All this, said Isaiah, was in the mind of God for Israel—a prophecy only finally fulfilled in the coming of Jesus Christ.

This was the most wonderful part of Isaiah's vision of hope for the people of Israel, and although the nation never lived up to the ideal of what Isaiah called the 'suffering servant', yet the idea lived on—and this mission was finally fulfilled in Jesus Christ the Son of God who was the perfect servant of God—the only one who could really make Isaiah's prophecy come true.

So with the days of exile coming to an end, the people of Israel prepared once more to return to their homeland. They had seen a great hope of the future while they had been in exile. They had suffered and had been forgiven. The two prophets—Ezekiel and Isaiah—had lifted the people's eyes to new horizons and to new enterprises. One was the eagerness to rebuild the Temple—but above all in many Hebrew hearts there was born the greater hope of One who would come to serve and lead them as the Holy One of God—the Messiah—a hope which eventually came to pass in the person of Jesus of Nazareth, the Son of God. *Ezekiel 3, 37–43; Isaiah 42–62*

11 PEOPLE OF THE HOMECOMING

Sing and rejoice, O daughter of Zion; for lo, I come and I will dwell in the midst of you, says the Lord. And many nations shall join themselves to the Lord in that day, and shall be my people; and I will dwell in the midst of you.

Zechariah 2. 10–11.

Homewards they went from Babylon.

THE NEWS soon spread that the great emperor Cyrus, King of Persia and master of all the lands watered by the famous rivers—Tigris and Euphrates—had given permission for the Hebrews to return home.

Cyrus dreamed of an empire which had many religions, many temples, many gods, but with only one ruler. The little lands of Judah and Israel were only a small part of his vast empire. He saw that these Hebrews were devoted to their God Yahweh and were eager to be in his holy place once again. So Cyrus gave the order that those who wished to do so could go home.

Not every Hebrew family was eager to make the long journey back to Jerusalem. Some of the people, after seventy years of living in the land of Babylon, were too old to move again. Some were too young to know what Jerusalem meant to their fathers and mothers, while many others had intermarried and had made their permanent homes in Babylon.

But many thousands of the people with hundreds of camels, horses, mules and donkeys did go back to their old home. Led by the priests and the senior men of the tribes the people marched in their family groups, each family carrying its possessions.

The priests carried the most precious things of all—the rich gold and silver vessels which Nebuchadnezzar had carried off from the old Temple. King Cyrus brought these splendid vessels from his treasury, and gave them to the priests to enrich the new Temple in Jerusalem.

To build the Temple again was the chief hope of the homecoming Hebrews. They dreamed of the Temple's past glories, but how disappointed the old people were when the foundations were laid! Many of them wept when they realized that they could not bring back the days of Solomon, but the younger ones shouted for joy as the foundations were dug.

BUILDING THE TEMPLE

Then began the long task of building the Temple itself. It was a hard and skilled job to carve the great stones, and to shape the huge timbers, but it was even harder to deal with those who objected to the newcomers doing it all themselves. Some of the

Hebrews who had not gone into exile felt that they should share in the building, and away in Persia the king wondered whether he had done right in allowing the Temple to be rebuilt at all.

But two prophets arose in Jerusalem to encourage the rebuilding: Haggai and Zechariah, whose books of prophecy are placed near the end of the Old Testament. 'Go up to the mountains and get the wood,' said Haggai. 'You are all building houses for yourselves,' he said, 'but my house must come first.'

Spurred on by the two prophets and by encouraging messages from Babylon, the Temple was finally finished, not so splendid as Solomon's but worthy of the God they worshipped, and for seven days the people feasted and worshipped in the place their fathers worshipped in.

The people marched in family groups—towards Jerusalem.

Soon after the Temple was finished, a further group of exiles returned from Babylon led by the priest Ezra. He came with the authority of the Persian king with much silver and gold, and many bullocks and rams for sacrificing. Ezra's mission was to remind the people once again of the 'law and the Covenant' which God had sworn with them through Moses. His mission was also to see that in the new Temple the exact ritual of worship was observed. For Ezra saw that the company of Hebrews after years of captivity needed discipline and training in their worship of God.

About the same time as Ezra, came an even greater leader Nehemiah from the land of Babylon. He had heard that the walls of the Holy City were still unbuilt, and he set to work to rebuild the walls. Gathering his team of builders, Nehemiah gave every one of them a sword to defend himself as he worked, for many local people objected to Nehemiah's plan.

At the call of the silver trumpet.

RESTORING THE WALLS

To the sound of trumpets, Nehemiah's men worked to restore the walls so that the Holy City should be truly a city once more. Nehemiah and Ezra set the Hebrews once more in their old home. They had the Temple. They had the City. They had their God to worship. They had the Law. But was that all that God was asking them to do in their homecoming? Had they learned any new lessons in captivity? Had they seen any vision of their God, as the God of all the world and of all people as well as the Hebrews?

Those questions were in the minds of many devout Hebrews at this time and many of them understood the meaning of the story of Jonah which began to be told among the people in Jerusalem.

JONAH'S MISSION

Jonah, happy in his life in Jerusalem, heard the word of God telling him to go to Nineveh to preach to that great and wicked city which needed to hear the call to repent. Jonah refused to listen and joined a ship going from Joppa to Tarshish. The ship sailed with Jonah on board and ran into a great storm. The sea was so mighty that the little ship threatened to break up and everyone on board cried to his god to save them— all except Jonah. He had gone to sleep in the inner part of the ship. The captain came to awake him and said to him.

'What do you mean, you sleeper? Get up, call on your God to help us.'

The storm blew, the ship rocked and the sailors grew more and more frightened. Someone in the ship was bringing this evil on them. Who could it be? They cast lots to discover who it was and the lot fell on Jonah.

Then they began to question Jonah about his country, his occupation and why he had come on to the ship. Where did he intend to go? What was he doing? Jonah had to confess that he was running away from God. He was refusing to do what God wanted him to do.

'Take me up,' said Jonah, 'and throw me into the sea. I know that it is because of me that this great storm is blowing. It is because I am refusing to do what God wants me to do. Throw me into the sea.'

The crew were reluctant to throw Jonah overboard. They rowed hard to bring the ship to land, but the sea only grew more and more tempestuous. So they heaved Jonah overboard, and the storm ceased.

In the sea Jonah was swallowed up by a great fish, which after three days cast him up on dry land and then he went on to Nineveh to preach.

The King of Nineveh and all his people listened to Jonah. They repented and fasted. But Jonah went away and sulked in anger. Why should God be merciful to this wicked city? Why should God forgive Nineveh? Jonah sat outside the city under a gourd tree which suddenly sprang up to give him shade, and then by next day withered and died. Jonah felt sorry for the plant, but his heart was not touched by the people of Nineveh. Then God asked him why he should not be merciful to Nineveh which had repented of its sin.

'Throw me overboard,' cried Jonah.

Jonah learned the lesson that all Israel was beginning to learn, that their God had pity and forgiveness for all people and not for Israel only. He was a God concerned with all the human family and not of the Hebrews only, and when men repented and turned to him he was merciful and forgiving. Jonah was Israel's missionary story.

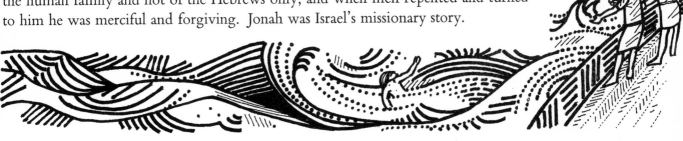

THE STORY OF JOB

Job too was another happy, prosperous man whose story the Israelites loved to re-tell and to puzzle over its lessons.

Job obeyed all the laws of God, and did no evil, and yet everything seemed to go wrong with him.

Job was blameless, righteous and honourable, but there descended upon him all the worst things that could happen. He became covered with sores from head to foot, his cattle and sheep died, raiders stole his camels, and the young people of his family perished in a storm.

In all his misery, Job argued with himself and his friends the deep questions of life. He asked: Is there any hope in life? Is there any wisdom, any truth, or is life all emptiness leading to nothing?

Job found no comfort among his friends but at last he found a new beginning for his life by a renewed trust in God whose ways are past all human understanding, and who is almighty and everlasting. Like the people of Israel, Job learned through hard and bitter experiences of life, to trust God.

Haggai 1; *Zechariah* 1; *Ezra* 8–10; *Nehemiah* 2–4; *Jonah*; *Job*

12 DREAMING OF THE FUTURE

And behold, with the clouds of heaven
there came one like a son of man . . . ,
And to him was given dominion
and glory and kingdom,
that all peoples, nations, and languages
should serve him;
his dominion is an everlasting dominion,
which shall not pass away,
and his kingdom one
that shall not be destroyed.

Daniel 7. 13–14.

THE GREAT image of gold was ten feet high and eight feet wide. It glittered in the hot sun of Babylon, and King Nebuchadnezzar was so proud of his wonderful idol that everybody in his kingdom, from the highest to the lowest, was commanded to worship it.

Everyone worshipped the golden god— except the three young men.

But it was reported to the king that certain young Hebrews—Shadrach, Meshach and Abednego—who were in the king's service, refused to worship the golden image because they believed in Yahweh, the High God.

'If it is true,' said the king, 'that these men refuse to worship, let them be thrown into a burning, fiery furnace and make the furnace seven times as hot.'

'Bind them, hand and foot, and throw them into the furnace. Let them perish in the flames.' But to the king's consternation the young men stood unharmed in the midst of the flames and as he watched he saw a fourth figure like an angel of God standing with them guarding them from harm.

In the fiery furnace—
not a hair was singed.

Then going to the furnace door, Nebuchadnezzar ordered the young men to come out, and saw that not a hair of their heads was singed, their clothes were not burned and there was no smell of fire on them at all.

'Blessed be the God of Shadrach, Meshach and Abednego,' said Nebuchadnezzar, 'who has delivered his servants who trusted in him and gave their bodies to be burned rather than serve and worship another god except their own God.' And the king promoted them in his service.

Having been in the fires of exile in Babylon, the older people of the Hebrews loved this story of the three faithful young men. They also loved all the other wonderful stories in the Book of Daniel which spoke of the courage and faith of the Hebrew people. Kings and empires might rise and fall, but the covenant between the Hebrew people and their God would last for ever.

The people of God had lived through the power of many empires—Egypt, Assyria, Babylon and Persia—and now the new empires of Greece and Rome were beginning to dominate their lives. Their faith was being threatened by new religions and new ways of life. They were in the fiery furnace of trouble and persecution once again—and even in the den of lions like Daniel.

In Babylon Daniel prayed three times a day to his God. He opened the window of his house towards Jerusalem and gave thanks to God. King Darius had forbidden anyone to pray except to himself. All the governors of his kingdom, of whom Daniel was a favourite one, had agreed to this law of the Medes and Persians, and Daniel knew it could not be changed, and that the penalty was to be thrown to the lions.

King Darius declared himself a god.

AMONG THE LIONS

But Daniel prayed regularly to God, until at last he was reported to the king, who commanded him to be thrown into the lions' den.

'May your God preserve you,' said King Darius, 'I am bound by the law I have made. I cannot change it even for you.'

Early in the morning the king went to the lions' den and instead of finding the mangled remains of Daniel he saw him there alive and walking about among the lions. Then King Darius made a decree that in all his kingdom men were to respect and honour the God of Daniel,

> For he is the living God,
>   enduring for ever;
> His kingdom shall never be destroyed,
>   and his dominion shall be to the end.   *Daniel 6. 26*

That was the hope and dream of the Hebrew people as the Old Testament closed its long account of God and his chosen people. The Book of Daniel showed them how Daniel and his friends were true and loyal in the days of exile in Babylon; they too must have the same faith in their day.

Like Daniel in his book, the people dreamed of the future. They had passed through the valley of suffering and death, but in all the fiery furnaces and the dens of lions, they kept on believing in the hope of the future. The old empires were passing and a new world was being born.

Daniel's God was greater than Darius— he ruled lions as well as men.

THE KINGDOM OF PEACE

In his visions Daniel had seen four great beasts representing the empires of the world, and these empires would one day be destroyed. Daniel's visions and prophecies pointed the people of Israel forward into the future when the kingdoms of this world would be replaced by God's everlasting kindom. Daniel looked to the time when the warring empires would destroy themselves by fighting, and to the day when 'those who are wise shall shine like the brightness of the firmament; and those who turn many to righteousness, like the stars for ever and ever.'

In all this turmoil and catastrophe how could the little land of Israel and the tiny nation of Hebrews be a light to the whole world? How could they match the splendour and might of the great empires? How could their God be the God of all mankind?

These are the questions on which the Old Testament brings its story forward to the fulfilment of its dream, that God would one day reveal himself to all men.

The flash of lightning and the roll of thunder are seen and heard in the Book of Daniel as the prophet looks forward to what God will do. The struggle between darkness and light will be fought out to the end, and then God will reign in his triumphant

Kingdom of Peace—a dream and hope which the Hebrew people never forsook, and which today they still look for.

This Kingdom of Light, Hope and Peace will dawn with the coming of the Son of Man to whom is given authority over all kingdoms and nations. His dominion will never pass away and all the peoples of the earth will serve him. On that note the Old Testament brings its panorama of people close to the New Testament's good news of Jesus Christ, who also bore the name of Son of Man. *Daniel 2–4, 6–7*

Someone will come!
The dream and hope
of Israel.

13 THE CHILD IS BORN

And Joseph also went up from Galilee, from the city of Nazareth, to Judea, to the city of David, which is called Bethlehem, because he was of the house and lineage of David, to be enrolled with Mary, his betrothed, who was with child. And while they were there, the time came for her to be delivered. And she gave birth to her first-born son and wrapped him in swaddling cloths, and laid him in a manger, because there was no place for them in the inn.

Luke 2. 4–7.

THE DONKEY stumbled along on the rough road. It had been a long journey, and the little animal, like its rider, was tired. From the donkey's back Mary looked eagerly ahead to catch the first glimpse of Bethlehem before the early darkness fell. By her side walked Joseph with one hand on the donkey's bridle and the other to steady Mary in the saddle.

From their home in Nazareth of Galilee, Mary, Joseph and the donkey had come seventy miles to Bethlehem in Judea, through the rough pathways of the Jordan valley and over the stony hills of Judea, and were now nearing Bethlehem.

Bethlehem was Joseph's home town where his family belonged, although he now lived far away in Nazareth. It was to Bethlehem that he had come to register his name in the census which the Roman governor had ordered.

As darkness fell, the lights began to glimmer in Bethlehem, and the tired travellers longed for the warmth and comfort of the inn. But Joseph soon discovered that Bethlehem was crowded with visitors who, like himself, had come to be registered. With Mary on the donkey he went from inn to inn asking for a place to sleep in the guest room. But all the rooms were full. All he could get was the offer of a bed among the hay in an inn stable.

There Joseph made a bed for Mary, and a place too for the faithful donkey. There he and Mary made ready for the event they had often talked of during the journey—the birth of Mary's baby.

THE GREAT SECRET

For Mary the babe in her arms in the stable at Bethlehem was the climax of a story of wonder and miracle. It began before she was married to Joseph, with the announce-

The baby of Bethlehem was the answer to Israel's hope.

No room for the Son of God.

ment to her by God that she should bear a son and that his name should be Jesus. The message about her son was this:

> He will be great, and will be called
>   the Son of the Most High;
> and the Lord God will give to him
>   the throne of his father David,
> and he will reign over the house of
>   Jacob for ever;
> and of his kingdom there will be
>   no end.
>
> *Luke* 1. 32–33

Mary told this great secret to her cousin Elizabeth, who, when she heard it, exclaimed excitedly, 'Blessed are you among women.' Elizabeth herself was about to have a son who became John the Baptist. The two women rejoiced together over the coming of their sons and Mary sang:

> My soul magnifies the Lord,
> and my spirit rejoices in God my Savior,
> for he has regarded the low estate of his handmaiden.
> For behold, henceforth all generations will call me
>   blessed;
> for he who is mighty has done great things for me,
> and holy is his name.
>
> *Luke* 1. 46–49

The remembrance of all this passed through Mary's mind as she lay there among the hay in the stable holding her baby son. She wondered about him, and dreamed of his future. Was he the Child the prophets had spoken about? Was he the One who would deliver Israel? Was this the Child for whom her people had been waiting for years?

Other watchers that night in Bethlehem also wondered about the new-born babe.

THE SHEPHERDS' VISION

Out on the hills round Bethlehem there were shepherds guarding their sheep from the night attacks of wild animals. In the quiet of the night as the sheep lay safely in the fold, the shepherds saw a bright light in the sky, and an angel came to them.

This is his star! Let us follow it to Bethlehem.

'Be not afraid,' said the angel. 'I bring you good news of a great joy which will come to all people; for to you is born this day in the city of David a Saviour who is Christ the Lord.'

The city of David! That meant Bethlehem, their own town!

Suddenly the heavens appeared to open and the shepherds and their sheep were enveloped in a 'multitude of the heavenly host' and the quiet hillside was filled with a heavenly choir singing:

> Glory to God in the highest,
> and on earth peace among men.

As the music and the singing died away, the shepherds looked at one another in amazement. Was this a dream? Was all this in their imagination? No. It must be true. They were shepherds of Bethlehem, and the word of the angel was that the child would be born in Bethlehem.

So as the early light of dawn came faintly over the hills, the shepherds left their sheep in the fold and hurried down to Bethlehem. They made enquiries at the various inns and finally were led to the stable where Mary and Joseph were with the child.

Looking at the child, the shepherds fell down to worship him, the forerunners of millions of humble people who have worshipped Jesus as the Eternal Son of God. Then they excitedly told the story of what happened in the hills among their sheep, of the light in the heavens and the singing of the angels, and the promise that the Child of Bethlehem was truly Christ the Lord.

Mary listened to all this exciting news, and held the baby tightly in her arms, as the shepherds worshipped her son as the Child of promise, the Child of hope, the one who would be King of all men and Saviour of mankind.

THE WISE MEN WORSHIP

To the stable where he lay.

Away over the hills in Jerusalem King Herod himself was startled to receive news of the new baby from three wise men.

'We have seen his star in the East, and have come to worship him,' said the wise men to King Herod.

'Whose star have you been following?' asked Herod.

'The star of Christ who is to be born King of the Jews.'

Herod was alarmed at the news, for under the Roman Emperor he alone was King of the Jews. Could there be another king? Could the age-old dream of the Jews be coming true? He knew the stars were said to tell their secrets to wise men. Could this be the star heralding the Christ, the Messiah?

Quickly he called a meeting of the priests and learned men and asked them what the prophets of old had prophesied about the birth of the Messiah. Where was it to be?

'In Bethlehem,' came the answer.

Then Herod hurried back to the wise men and told them to follow their star, and see whether it led them to Bethlehem, and to let him know immediately when the child was born.

'Go and search diligently for the child,' said Herod, 'that I too may come and worship him.'

The star shone brilliantly in the night sky as the wise men moved down the road from Jerusalem. It twinkled in the deep darkness, clearly leading them to the place where the child was. Even their camels seemed to follow the star leading towards Bethlehem.

Coming into the narrow streets of the town, the wise men were surprised to find them crowded, and the inns overfull. Where was the child in this crowded city? Where was the child's home, the child's parents? Where could his mother be?

Questions like these were answered for the wise men by the star, which seemed to shine and twinkle more brightly over one area of Bethlehem.

There the wise men heard of a woman and her husband who had been compelled to sleep in a stable because the inn was so crowded. There the woman had given birth to a child.

Their guiding star was still steadily shining above them as they entered the stable. Moving into the dimly-lit little place, they could see a woman sitting among the hay. In her arms she held a baby.

Behind the mother stood a man attentive, listening, watching. A donkey lifted its head as the men stood for a moment in silent admiration and then fell on their knees to worship. Opening their treasures, they offered him gifts, gold and frankincense and myrrh.

In the days of King Herod.

PROTECTING THE CHILD

The news from the wise men about King Herod warned Joseph that he should take special care of the new-born babe. According to Matthew's Gospel the wise men did not go back to tell King Herod of their discovery and Joseph took Mary and the child down to Egypt for safety.

King Herod was angry when he saw that he had been tricked by the wise men. The child who might rival him as King of the Jews was still living, perhaps somewhere in Bethlehem! How could he be sure that the child would not be used by his enemies to set up a rival kingdom?

In his dark, evil mind, Herod planned a cruel deed. He sent an order to the authorities at Bethlehem that, for the sake of the security of the kingdom, all male children of two years of age and under living in Bethlehem at the time of the wise men's visit should be killed. This monstrous deed was carried out bringing grief and misery to many Bethlehem homes.

To be safe from Herod, they went down to Egypt.

Meanwhile in Egypt, Joseph, Mary and Jesus waited for news of Herod's death, so that they might all go home in safety to live in Nazareth.

When the news came, Joseph made preparations for the journey. He was a poor man and the journey had to be on foot, with Mary and the child riding on a donkey. All through the hard, sandy, desert country Joseph guided the donkey bearing its precious burden.

The stories of the Hebrew past were strongly fixed in Joseph's mind as the donkey trudged on under the hot sun, for he was proud of belonging to the family of King David. He liked to think of the great past of his people, and how they had come out of Egypt into the Promised Land. He liked to think of the great hope that one day the Messiah, the king, would lead the Jewish people. Like his ancestors Joseph too was going home, but unlike them Joseph carried with him the secret of the future of his people. The secret lay there in Mary's arms.

THE CHILD IN THE TEMPLE

According to Luke's Gospel Joseph and Mary eventually brought the child Jesus into the Temple to present him to God. All Hebrew baby boys were brought in this way into the Temple. Mary and Joseph were anxious to obey every part of the law so that Jesus when he grew up would be recognized as a devout member of the Jewish people. They made their offerings too of a pair of doves, as was the Jewish custom.

Coming into the Temple with the child, Mary and Joseph noticed an old man standing in the court. He was well known to the priests and Temple authorities as Simeon, a devout Jew who prayed and hoped for the coming of the Messiah. Indeed, old though he was, Simeon had been promised in a vision that he should not die until he had seen the Messiah. He came regularly to the Temple, believing that one day God would reveal to him the great secret of the Messiah.

Simeon watched Mary and Joseph with the child in Mary's arms as they came into the courtyard, and felt impelled to go towards Mary and to take the child into his arms. Mary watched the old man's face. It glowed with delight, sending out a kind of divine radiance. Simeon held the child close to him, and then, lifting him up so that Mary and Joseph and all the people could see and hear, Simeon broke into a hymn of thanksgiving:

> Lord, now lettest thou thy servant
>   depart in peace,
> according to thy word;
> for mine eyes have seen thy salvation
> which thou hast prepared in the presence
>   of all peoples,
> a light for revelation to the Gentiles,
> and for a glory to thy people Israel.

Luke 2. 29–32

'I have seen the Light of the World.'

Simeon's hymn of thanksgiving attracted the attention of another person who also prayed regularly in the Temple for the coming of the Messiah. It was Anna, an old lady of great age who was said to stay perpetually in the Temple courtyard fasting and praying. Like Simeon, she too gave thanks to God at the sight of the child Jesus.

HOME IN NAZARETH

In Nazareth, Jesus grew up in the home of Joseph the carpenter. It was twelve years before he was again in the Temple, twelve long years of his boyhood of which we know nothing except that, according to St Luke, he 'grew and became strong, filled with wisdom, and the favour of God was upon him'.

But in his twelfth year, Joseph and Mary brought him again to the Temple at the time of the Passover feast. They came in company with many other Nazareth people, and after the celebrations the pilgrims started off homewards—but Jesus was missing.

'Where is Jesus?' Mary's anxious question was passed through the company on the road to Galilee.

'Where is Jesus?' Mary thought he might be with their friends and kinsfolk. Everyone looked for him but he was not to be found.

Mary and Joseph turned wearily back to Jerusalem. They had gone a day's journey towards Galilee, so three days passed before they found Jesus in the Temple sitting among the learned men, listening to them and asking them questions. Everyone was astonished at the boy, at his understanding and his answers, but Mary could only think of the trouble Jesus had caused his family and friends.

'Son,' she said 'Why have you treated us so? We have been looking for you every-where.'

'But how is it,' replied Jesus, 'that you did not know that I must be about my father's business?'

My father's business! That saying puzzled Joseph and Mary as they left the Temple with Jesus to catch up with their friends, now far on the road to Nazareth. My father's business! Mary wondered what Jesus meant. It could only mean his heavenly Father. Mary wondered and wondered at the phrase and kept the saying secret in her own heart. Jesus came home with Joseph and Mary to Nazareth and was obedient to them.

Matthew 2; Luke 2

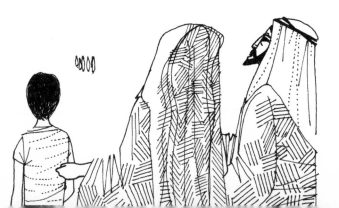

*Home to Nazareth
again.*

14 HERALD OF GOD

In those days came John the Baptist, preaching in the wilderness of Judea, 'Repent, for the kingdom of heaven is at hand.' For this is he who was spoken of by the prophet Isaiah when he said, 'The voice of one crying in the wilderness: Prepare the way of the Lord, make his paths straight.' *Matthew 3. 1–3.*

'HE'S DOWN there by the Jordan, living on locusts and wild honey.' So ran the news in the streets of Jerusalem about John the Baptist. People began to wonder about this strange man down there by the river.

'Who is he?' they asked.

'A prophet! A man of God! It may be the Messiah himself? Who knows?' was the answer.

The gossip in Jerusalem was confused and the shops and inns were full of rumours.

'He wears a camel-hair skin with a leather girdle. He baptizes people in the river. He foretells the future. He speaks of someone who is to come after him—someone mighty and important,' ran the news.

So the crowds by the river began to increase. From Jerusalem down the steep roads to the Jordan there was a steady stream of people, some curious to see the latest sight, others bent on hearing this strange man—and all of them fascinated by this prophet who had come out of the wilderness to preach his gospel of repentance.

The strange figure down by the Jordan.

NEWS WORTH HEARING

Many said they had heard it all before. It was the same message as the prophets of old had preached. Repentance? Yes. They had heard all about that.

But what was this that the prophet was saying about someone 'coming after me whose sandals I am not worthy to carry'?

This was news worth hearing.

So the people flocked round John on the banks of the Jordan. Not only city people from Jerusalem, but countrymen from the farms and vineyards of the Jordan valley gathered in the hot and humid atmosphere. There was the Jordan flowing slowly past on its way to the Dead Sea, and there on its bank stood this strange figure of John the Baptist dressed in camel hair with a leather girdle about his waist.

'Repent and be baptized. The kingdom of heaven is at hand,' cried John.

'Come and be baptized.' He went down into the river and many people followed him to be baptized, confessing their sins. But when John saw some of the religious leaders from Jerusalem joining the crowds on the river bank, he warned them not to

75

hide behind their traditions. Not even Abraham could save them from God's anger if they did not sincerely repent. The time of harvest is coming, he warned. Then the good wheat will be gathered into the barns and the chaff burnt in the fire.

'There is one coming,' said John, 'who will baptize with the Holy Spirit and with fire. I am his forerunner, his messenger. I come to prepare his way, to make his paths straight.'

'Are you Elijah?' they asked, or 'are you the prophet who is to come? Who are you?'

WATCH FOR HIS COMING

'I am not the Christ,' said John. 'I am the voice of one crying in the wilderness. I am sent to make straight the way of the Lord. There is one among you whom you do not yet know. He is to come after me. Watch for him.'

'What shall we do?' asked the people. 'How shall we repent?' 'Tell us what to do,' they pleaded as they thronged round John. 'Give us a plan for repentance.'

John looked out over the crowd of people—farmers, soldiers, shop-keepers, government officials. Many of them had stood with him in the river to be baptized. Now they wanted to know exactly how they should change their way of living.

To tell them to keep to the Hebrew traditions faithfully was not enough. John knew that he was the forerunner of a Gospel which would cut at the roots of all the old Hebrew ways of living. The one who was coming after him would preach a new way of life for every man.

'Here is your plan for repentance,' he said.

'Every man who has two coats let him share with him who has none. He who has plenty of food let him share with the hungry.'

Turning to the government officials in the crowd, and especially those who collected the taxes from the people, John spoke a very practical word. He knew that many of the tax-collectors got more money out of the people than they were entitled to. They were hated by all. 'You tax-collectors,' said John, 'collect no more than is your right.'

The soldiers asked what they should do. John's answer for them was, 'Rob no one by violence or by false accusation, and be content with your wages.'

76

All Jerusalem flocked to the river—and Jesus came too.

THE NEW LIFE

These practical answers for practically-minded people showed John's listeners that repentance was not just a form of words. For him baptism meant the start of a new life. He was the forerunner of a new way of righteousness and justice.

For many of his listeners, John was an echo of Isaiah the prophet:

> The voice of one crying in the wilderness:
> Prepare the way of the Lord,
> make his paths straight.

But others saw in him the signs of the expected Messiah. Rumours ran round Jerusalem that 'the prophet', the 'expected one', had already arrived in the Jordan valley. But every time John heard this rumour he pointed to the One who was about to come. He did not know the exact time or place. He only knew that in preparation for the coming men should repent and turn to God.

It was then that Jesus himself came into the Jordan valley from his home in Galilee. He too had heard of John and his preaching, for the fame of the prophet had spread through all the land. He knew that this was the moment for him to begin his ministry. John's preaching had prepared the way for him—the Young Man of Galilee—to begin his mission for God.

Whether Jesus had already been in touch with John we do not know. It may have been that, related as cousins through their mothers Mary and Elizabeth, they had already met. But, as the Gospels relate the story, the visit of Jesus to John was a surprise.

John saw Jesus coming towards him on the river bank. Among the crowd of people there was no mistaking him as he walked slowly up to John. But only John knew that it really was Jesus.

Pointing to Jesus, John said, 'I need to be baptized by you. Why do you come to me?'

'Let it be done now,' said Jesus 'for it is right to perform righteous acts.' So Jesus went down into the Jordan with John and stood in the water for his baptism. As he came up out of the water, the heavens appeared to open, and a voice came from out of the cloud, 'This is my beloved Son, with whom I am well pleased.'

For John this was the climax of his prophecy. For Jesus it was the beginning of his ministry. The Young Man of Galilee was baptized and prepared.

Matthew 3. 1–12; *Mark* 1. 2–9; *Luke* 3. 10–21

15 YOUNG MAN OF GALILEE

And he went about all Galilee, teaching in their synagogues and preaching the gospel of the kingdom and healing every disease and every infirmity among the people. So his fame spread throughout all Syria, and they brought him all the sick, those afflicted with various diseases and pains, demoniacs, epileptics, and paralytics, and he healed them.

Matthew 4. 23–24.

THERE WERE people everywhere in Galilee—in the villages, on the farms, by the lake-shore. In Nazareth, where Jesus lived, and away down on the lake at Capernaum, people lived in small towns and worked as craftsmen, inn-keepers, traders and fishermen. No big capital cities, no great main roads, and no great men and houses dominated the life of Galilee. Nazareth was far away from the main centres of Jewish life, but in its fold of the Galilean hills it was a lively little place with all the friendliness and intimacies of village life.

People set out with their donkeys to visit their friends, to do business, to go to

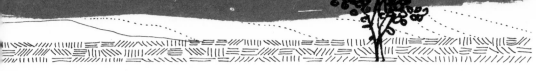

weddings and funerals. In the bright morning sunshine, pathways across the hills usually had groups of travellers going to vineyards on the hillsides, or to the fishing villages on the lake-shore. In the springtime they could see the farmer sowing his seed, scattering it by hand across the ploughed field, and in the summer the reapers and gleaners were busy in the harvest fields.

Down by the shore of the Sea of Galilee lived the fishermen, boat-builders, net-makers, fish-sellers. It was always warm down there, six hundred feet below sea-level, and in summertime the heat was almost unbearable. The fishermen of Galilee did good business, for fish were plentiful in the lake and they could get high prices for their catches.

No one expected anything very wonderful to happen in Galilee. Far away from the great cities, its life was very simple, linked to the round of the farming seasons. Seed-time and harvest made the pattern of Galilean life. But there was one other influence in Galilee, and that was the synagogue.

In most large villages the synagogue was at the heart of the community. This was the Sabbath meeting-place for worship, where the law of Moses was recited, and the prophets were read. The synagogue was the meeting-place of the people, but it was also a school where the children learned the law and were taught the customs of the people. There was no ordained minister in the synagogue. Anyone with sufficient learning, judged suitable, could be asked to read and to preach the sermon.

Galilee—a land of fishermen and farmers.

IN THE SYNAGOGUE

That was why one Sabbath morning Jesus read the Scriptures and preached the sermon in the Nazareth synagogue.

All eyes were fixed on him. They knew him as a boy in the village, as assistant to Joseph in his carpenter's shop. He had had no more education than any other boy in the village, but there was something about him which was different.

He stood up to read from the prophet Isaiah:

> The Spirit of the Lord is upon me,
> because he has anointed me to preach
> good news to the poor.
> He has sent me to proclaim release
> to the captives
> and recovering of sight to the blind,
> to set at liberty those who are oppressed
> to proclaim the acceptable year of the Lord.

When he had finished reading, the eyes of all in the synagogue were fixed on him. They had all heard this Scripture read before, but never like this. It seemed as if this young man, Jesus, was claiming that what the Scripture said was coming true through him. He not only read the Scriptures, but he turned the reading into an announcement about himself as the king who would reign and bring in God's kingdom.

All the people were staggered at the idea. Then their surprise turned to admiration that one of their own young men should be saying this. Was this just Joseph's son? Was this the boy they knew in Nazareth?

They listened eagerly as Jesus went on to speak about the meaning of God's kingdom. He described how Elijah found food and drink outside Israel in the land of Sidon, and that Elisha healed even the non-Jewish general Naaman of his leprosy. 'The Jews,' he said, 'were not the only people within the kingdom. God cared for all people wherever they lived and whatever their race.'

Everyone's eyes were fixed on him.

All this was too much for the Nazareth congregation. They could only think of themselves, their own needs and their own Jewish ways of life. A wave of anger swept through the synagogue at the thought that one of their own young men should preach like this. Why could he not think of Nazareth and its needs first?

The whole congregation rose to throw him out of the building. Outside the mob seized him and led him to the top of a hill to hurl him headlong. But Jesus escaped into safety.

DOWN BY THE LAKE

As the news about Jesus spread, people down by the lake were all agog when he came along the shore. What good could come out of Nazareth? they wondered. Were all the stories about this Jesus true? Could he work the wonders they had heard about? These hardy fishermen of Lake Galilee were not easily moved by the news coming over the hills from Nazareth. They would wait and see.

Jesus came along the shore of the lake and stood watching two fishermen casting their nets into the water. The men stood knee-deep in the water with the huge net swirling round them as they threw it with all their might to make a catch.

They watched Jesus and waited for him to speak.

'*Fish for men,' he said.*

'Follow me,' he said, 'and I will make you become fishers of men.'

The two brothers, Peter and Andrew, immediately left their nets and stood with Jesus on the shore. They followed him as he led the way to the next two fishermen who were in their boat mending their nets.

These two brothers, James and John, worked with their father, Zebedee, but as soon as Jesus called them, they too left their boat and the nets with their father and followed Jesus.

With these four men as his first friends Jesus began to preach the good news of the kingdom of God. People flocked to hear him as they did to John the Baptist. On one occasion there were so many of them that Jesus sat in one of Simon Peter's boats and asked him to push the boat out a little way from the shore. With the boat as his pulpit, Jesus spoke to the people on the shore.

But all the time he was speaking, Simon Peter was troubled in his heart about the bad fishing they had had that night.

'Master,' he said, 'we fished all night and caught nothing.'

'Put out into the lake,' said Jesus, 'and let down your nets and see what happens.'

They let down their great nets into the lake, and, as soon as they began to draw them, their net broke down with the weight of fish, so that the boat began to sink.

'Don't be afraid,' said Jesus, 'think of people more than fish. From now on you can catch men, if you have faith to do it.'

81

In the towns and villages round the lake Jesus found many different kinds of people. One day, entering the town of Capernaum, he met a Roman centurion, the military officer in charge of the Roman soldiers in Capernaum.

'Master,' he said to Jesus, 'I have a servant lying at home, paralysed and helpless, and in terrible distress.'

Jesus was surprised that a Roman military officer should come to speak to him and immediately he said to the centurion, 'I will come to your house and heal him.'

'Master, I am not worthy to have you come under my roof. Say the word now and my servant will be healed. You have authority to do this. I too have authority of a different kind. My soldiers obey my orders and my slaves do as I tell them. But I believe you have the power to heal. I have faith that this can be done through you.'

Jesus was so surprised at the simple, deep faith of the Roman centurion, that he turned to his disciples and pointed out to them that this man was a Roman, and not a Jew. He had not been trained in the traditions of Abraham, Isaac and Jacob, but yet he believed, and there would be a place for him in God's kingdom.

'Go home,' he said to the centurion, 'and when you get there you will find your servant healed.'

'This is real faith,' said Jesus to his disciples, 'I have never found such faith among my own Jewish people.'

THE TAX-COLLECTOR

That Jesus should find friends among people like the Roman centurion shocked some people. They got a greater shock when he was seen one day talking to a man at the

Jesus talked with all kinds of people— even a Roman centurion.

He talked too with the hated tax-collector.

local tax office in Capernaum. Tax officials were bitterly hated by everyone, for they not only collected the taxes which were due to be paid, but often tried to collect a bit more to put in their own pockets. Most people avoided meeting anyone connected with the tax office. The crowd which followed Jesus through the streets of Capernaum were amazed when he stopped at the office and began to talk with the official sitting there with his papers and his files.

Jesus looked at the man, called him by his name, Matthew, and said, 'Follow me.'

To the astonishment of the onlookers, Matthew got up from his desk, brushed his papers aside and walked out to be with Jesus, and then led him into his house. The eyes of the onlookers opened even wider to see this Jesus of Nazareth, who appeared to be a Teacher or a Prophet, enter the house of a tax-collector.

'Look,' said some of the religious leaders who were watching the proceedings, 'your teacher goes into the house of a tax-collector. He should not be friendly with such sinners. He is even sitting down to eat with them. This is not done in our religion.'

'Why not?' asked Jesus. 'Why should I not go into Matthew's house? Why should I not have a meal with a tax-collector? I am here not to be with righteous people only but with sinners.'

'Think again,' said Jesus, 'and ask yourselves what a doctor does. He goes to those who need him, to the sick and people who are ill. Those who are fit and well do not need him. I am come to help those who need me.'

THE SICK WOMAN

Even when the crowds were thronging round him, Jesus was sensitive to people. He never let the big crowd take his mind away from the individual people who made up the crowd.

83

A sick woman once came up behind him in the street, as he walked along with the crowd following him. She was only one among scores of people who pressed close to him as he went along. They touched his clothes and came very close to him—but it was the touch of the woman that Jesus felt most of all.

'Who was it that touched me?' asked Jesus.

'Touched you, master?' said Peter, 'why, we all touched you. The crowd is pressing round you. You can't help being touched by scores of people.'

Jesus stood still in the midst of the people and looked round over the crowd.

'I know that power has gone out from me. Someone in particular touched me,' he said.

Then the woman pushed her way to the front and knelt before Jesus.

'I touched the fringe of your robe,' she said. 'I had faith that if only I could feel the hem of your garment I would be made well. At that very moment the flow of blood within me ceased and I felt well again. No doctor has been able to cure me.'

Jesus looked lovingly at the woman kneeling before him.

'Daughter,' he said, 'your faith has made you well: go in peace.'

He took the child by the hand.

THE DEAD ARE RAISED

Jesus made no distinction between the various kinds of people he met in Galilee. Some were poor, some rich. Some belonged to the ruling and educated groups, while others were humble and unlearned. Soon after he had healed the servant of the Roman centurion he was invited into the house of a Jewish ruler, an important man in the life of the synagogue and greatly respected among the Jews.

The ruler came to Jesus and knelt before him, which in itself was a remarkable act of recognition by an older man of position to such a young man as Jesus.

'My daughter has just died,' said the ruler, 'but if you will come and lay your hand on her she will live.'

It was the man's faith that drew Jesus to him. When he came to the house, the mourners were already wailing and crying—the flute players were making their doleful music and the whole place was in a hubbub of noise.

'Make way,' said Jesus, 'get out of the house. Let us have peace and quiet. I believe that the child is not dead but sleeping.' They all laughed, but Jesus went inside and took the child by the hand and she arose.

This power to raise the dead to life again was seen most dramatically when Jesus came into the village of Nain up on the hills not far from Nazareth. It may have been a village in which Jesus had many friends, and perhaps he knew the widow whose son had died. As he came into the village, Jesus met the sad procession with the bearers carrying the young man's body to be buried outside the village. He was the only son of his mother, and the whole village had turned out to accompany her in sympathy to the burial. She walked behind the bearers weeping at the loss of her son—a sight which moved Jesus deeply.

'Don't cry,' he said to her. He had compassion on the poor woman now left without the help and comfort of her only son. He knew what that meant for her—not only loneliness, but poverty. Without the help of her son, she might go hungry and even homeless.

'Do not weep,' he repeated.

He touched the bier. The bearers stood still and the whole crowd of weeping sorrowful people watched with pent emotion and wonder. What would he do?

In a clear voice so that everyone could hear, Jesus spoke to the young man on the bier.

'Young man, I say to you, arise.'

To the amazement of his mother and the crowd of villagers, the young man sat up and began to speak. The astonished bearers lowered the bier to the ground, and Jesus gave the young man back to his mother alive and well.

News about this Young Man of Galilee—this Jesus of Nazareth—reached all the villages and towns and the remote farms and vineyards. Wherever Galileans met, they passed on the news of the extraordinary happenings whenever Jesus was present. The blind could see again, the lame walked, lepers were healed, the deaf were cured and the dead raised up.

This was indeed wonderful news for all the people, and many thanked God that they had seen the power of the kingdom of God, displayed and used by Jesus. But others said it was the devil at work, and that Jesus was using evil powers to do good. The religious leaders, too, were critical and followed him round, hoping to catch him in some act which broke the Jewish law.

By the lake-shore with his disciples.

MASTER AND MEN

But in all these contacts with different people, Jesus never forgot his inner group of friends—his disciples. They walked with him along the paths of Galilee, through the fields of grain, the grassy stretches where the flowers bloomed, and along the lake-shore. They were the learners. He was the Teacher. They were his friends but he was the Master. He called them by their names—Peter and Andrew, James and John, Philip and Bartholomew, Matthew and Thomas, James and Simon, Judas the son of James, and Judas Iscariot who later betrayed Jesus. He grew to know them intimately.

Whenever the crowd was too great, they protected him. When he was tired, they found him a place to rest. They talked with him in their homes and listened to him as he spoke in the streets. They were always learning, wondering and believing.

85

'Only enough for ourselves,' they said.

But it was the crowds which came to him that concerned Jesus too. The Gospel story says he 'had compassion on them'. They seemed to be people without a leader, not knowing what to do and where to go. They followed him round Galilee into the hills and by the lake, listening to his teaching and bringing out their sick for him to heal—just ordinary people of the Galilee countryside who found in Jesus something that appealed to them. Here they saw a religious teacher who was different from all the other religious teachers. He cared for the people and spoke in clear, simple language. He used the incidents of everyday life to make the meaning of his message very real and understandable. All sorts of living people came into his parables—the sower, the fisherman, the woman at home, the merchant, the shopkeeper, bride and bridegroom, the widow, little children, mothers and fathers. Jesus spoke about life and how to live it. For the people of Galilee he made religion a practical, everyday experience.

No wonder the people followed Jesus even into the most remote parts of Galilee. In one lonely place, as evening came on, the disciples wanted to send the people away into the villages in order to buy food. The crowd had been with Jesus all day and had had little to eat, and the darkness was falling.

'Send them away,' said the disciples to Jesus.

'No,' replied Jesus, 'you give them food to eat.'

'But we have only five loaves and two fishes. Just enough for ourselves,' they said, 'how can we make that go round among so many?'

'Give me the food,' said Jesus, 'and tell the people to sit down on the grass.'

Then Jesus blessed the loaves and the fishes and began to distribute them to the disciples who gave the food to the people. Everyone was astonished to see that the food never gave out. The bread and the fish went round the whole crowd, which

numbered over five thousand people, and when they had finished eating there were enough broken pieces to fill twelve baskets.

No wonder that his disciples began to believe that the Young Man of Galilee was truly the Son of God.

Matthew 8. 5–26, 14. 16–21; Luke 4. 16–29, 7. 11–17

16 PEOPLE ROUND THE LAKE

> And when they had crossed over, they came to land at Gennesaret.
>
> *Matthew 14. 34.*

FROM WHERE he sat in the boat, just off the shore, Jesus could see the people and they could see him as well as hear him. The crowds thronged round him so much that he was forced to use the boat as a kind of pulpit. But his voice carried easily to the people on the shore.

Jesus could see over the heads of the people to the hills beyond the shore, where the farmers were at work. His eye caught the man sowing seed across the freshly ploughed land, and as the man sowed Jesus spoke a parable to the people.

'A sower,' he said, 'went out to sow, and as he sowed some seeds fell along the path, and the birds ate them up. Other seeds fell on rocky ground where there was not much soil and immediately they sprang up and grew. But they had no depth of soil and the sun soon scorched them. Some seeds fell among thorns which soon choked them, and some fell into good soil and brought forth a bountiful crop.'

'Anyone who sees the sower at work,' said Jesus, 'knows the meaning of the parable, for seeds are like people.'

Some people hear the truth of God but their interest soon fades away because other

Seeds are like people.

87

Small seed—big tree.

things become more important. Then there are people who are 'fine weather' believers. While all is going well they believe, but when trouble starts they give up. Other people find that the things of the world are more interesting and have no time for the truths of God. But there are people, like the good seed, who hear, understand, and bear fruit.

Jesus used his method of parable and story to help people understand his teaching. He used the homely illustrations which his listeners would immediately recognize.

'A mustard tree,' he said, 'is one of the big trees, but it grows from one of the tiniest seeds of all, and the "kingdom of God" is like that.'

'When a woman bakes bread, she puts yeast into the flour to make it rise. The yeast is hidden in the flour but it soon spreads its power everywhere—and that,' said Jesus, 'is how people who believe in God and his kingdom should work too.'

'If a merchant who buys and sells fine pearls discovers one pearl of great value, he will sell all his stock of pearls to buy this special one. The kingdom of God is like that,' he said. 'It is so valuable that it is worth giving up everything to be in it.'

MESSENGERS OF THE KINGDOM

It was to spread the news of the kingdom of God to the people that Jesus sent out his disciples. He gave them power and authority to heal and to preach, with careful instructions about their equipment and their methods.

'Don't clutter yourself with baggage,' he said, 'travel light. Take no bag, no stick, no bread, and no money. Just go as you are, and don't take even an extra coat.'

Jesus saw his disciples as messengers of the kingdom who would be welcomed wherever they went. Homes would be thrown open to give them lodging and food. They were to stay with friends in one place and not waste time moving about from house to house. If they could not find friends in one town they were to move on to the next.

So the disciples spread out through the villages and towns of Galilee carrying the news of the kingdom of God. They moved round the lake-shore and wherever they went people listened eagerly to their message that the kingdom of God had already come in the person of Jesus of Nazareth. Across the hills, through the farms and the vineyards, over the brow of the hills towards Nazareth, they went with the wonderful news.

People were surprised that these men had no money, and carried no food and were not burdened by baggage like other travellers. They were eager and enthusiastic, and their enthusiasm was infectious. These preachers were different from all others who had ever preached in Galilee, and the people flocked to hear them.

Jesus warned his messengers that they would not always be welcomed wherever they went. They had to be prepared for arrest, imprisonment, beatings, and even to be despised and rejected by their own families. 'But do not be afraid,' he said, 'and do not be worried about what you shall say. All that will be given you at the moment you need it.'

'He who receives you receives me, and he who receives me receives him who sent me'—that was the wonderful commission Jesus gave to his disciples as they set out to be his messengers. Anyone who helped them, even though it was only with a cup of cold water, Jesus promised would be amply rewarded.

They saw the paralysed man walk home.

THE PARALYSED MAN

Wherever he went round the lake of Galilee, Jesus was followed by people of all kinds—some curious to see what he would do; others critical of his actions; and all of them wondering where his power came from. Some people even made the long journey from Jerusalem, among them many religious leaders and teachers of the law.

On one occasion at Capernaum, the crowd was so great that Jesus went into a house to escape the press of the people, but the people—including Pharisees from Jerusalem—invaded the house, blocked the doorway and then surrounded the house. Knowing that Jesus was there, some friends of a paralysed man carried him along on his bed, determined to present him to Jesus. But every approach was thronged with people and there was no way to get into the house with a bed.

Then the paralysed man's friends hit upon an ingenious idea. Why not uncover the flat roof of the house and let down the bed with the man on it? They took off the light wood coverings, carried the man up the outside steps and with a couple of ropes gently lowered his bed into the middle of the room where Jesus was. Like everyone else in the room Jesus was astonished at the faith of the man and his friends, but his first words to him were, 'Man, your sins are forgiven you.'

Who is this that speaks in the name of God? thought the Pharisees. Only God is able to forgive sins!

But, knowing what was in their hearts, Jesus asked them which is easier to say, 'Your sins are forgiven you' or 'Rise and walk'. But to show his power over all life, Jesus also said to the man, 'Rise, take up your bed, and go home.' To the amazement of the crowd the man rose before them and took up his bed and walked.

THE SABBATH FOR MAN

Jesus was often in conflict with the Pharisees, because he seemed to do things which were not in strict keeping with the Jewish law. One day he and his disciples were walking through the grainfields, and the disciples began to pluck ears of grain to eat, for they were hungry. To the strictest Jew that meant working on the Sabbath, and the Pharisees were quick to point this out, and wondered how Jesus would answer their charge.

They also watched him in the synagogue on the Sabbath day. A man with a withered hand came up to Jesus. Would he heal him on the Sabbath? The Pharisees wondered. If he did, that would break the Sabbath law.

Jesus called the man to him and turning to the Pharisees he said, 'Is it lawful on the Sabbath to do good, or to do harm, to save life or to kill?' They had no answer, and Jesus was angry with them.

'If you would be great,' said Jesus, 'become like a child.'

'Stretch out your hand,' said Jesus, and immediately the man's withered hand was healed.

'The Sabbath,' said Jesus, 'is meant for man and not man for the Sabbath.' To do good on the Sabbath was not breaking the law, for people are more important than the Sabbath itself and to serve them is also to serve and honour God.

Jesus saw that the Jewish religious leaders worshipped the outward observances of their faith and forgot the inner meaning of what they did. They loved to be careful and accurate about many small details of their customs and traditions but often disregarded the spirit of the act. They loved the tradition itself rather than the people who followed it.

Even the disciples of Jesus were like this too. They asked Jesus on one occasion who would be the greatest in the kingdom of heaven. They thought that special places would be reserved for them because they had been close to Jesus. Like the Pharisees they thought that outward observance and position were very important in religion.

But Jesus, instead of arguing with them, did a very simple thing. Looking round the crowd his eye lighted on a child, and he called the child to him.

'Look,' he said, 'unless you turn and become like children, you will never enter into the kingdom of heaven. Whoever humbles himself like this child is the greatest in the kingdom of heaven.'

Become like children! That was a new idea for these tough and hardy fishermen, who expected a privileged place in the kingdom of their master. How could grown-up men become like children? Jesus led them to see that it was not outward importance that mattered in his kingdom but inward humility of spirit.

'He that is least among you all is the one who is great,' said Jesus. If a person wished to be important, then he had to learn how to be humble and unimportant, for Christ's kingdom is made up of people like that.

Jesus went on to tell his disciples that they should be careful not to despise people who seem unimportant.

'Anyone,' he said, 'who takes a little child in my name receives me, and if anyone should hurt a child in any way, it would be better for him to be drowned in the sea with a great millstone hanged round his neck!' Nothing was more important than people in the sight of God, and men had to show this in their relationships with one another.

Jesus put it all very clearly in the story of the shepherd and his sheep. He asked his disciples to think of a man with a hundred sheep out on the hillside. All day long the sheep fed quietly on the short, crisp grass among the rocks and in the gullies. As they fed, so the sheep scattered far and wide, and at evening when the shepherd gathered them into the fold there was one missing. He counted them again and again, but still it was only ninety-nine.

One sheep missing, somewhere on the hills! The shepherd's heart was troubled and anxious. He must find the sheep. This was the one he most cared for at the moment. The ninety-nine were safely in the fold—but this one was missing! He must find it. So off he went across the hills looking for it, and he was not happy until he found it.

'God's love is like that,' said Jesus. God cares for the individual person. He loves people—even the most unimportant, and his kingdom is made up of people of humble heart. There were to be no special privileges for anyone, not even for those who were closely related to himself.

Jesus made this plain one day when his mother and brothers came to see him. They just stood there in the crowd outside the house hoping that they might speak to him. A message was sent in to Jesus saying that they were waiting outside.

'Your mother and brothers wish to see you,' said the messenger.

Jesus thought for a moment and then said, 'My mother and my brothers are those who hear the word of God and do it.' Jesus was not turning his back on his own family, but reminding his disciples that in the kingdom of God all people were brothers and sisters. The ties of his family were very close for Jesus, but the ties of the greater family of God were even closer.

TRAINING THE DISCIPLES

Sheep are like people.

For Jesus the shores of Galilee were the training ground for the intimate friendship with his disciples. He knew that upon their understanding of him so much depended.

Three disciples—Peter, James and John—were more closely linked to Jesus than the rest. These three fishermen were with him constantly as he moved about Galilee and it was these that Jesus took with him to a high hill overlooking the lake. There in the quietness of the mountain, Jesus was transfigured before them and appeared in glistening white garments as he talked with the prophets Elijah and Moses.

Struck dumb by the vision of Jesus on the mountain, the disciples heard a voice out of the over-shadowing cloud,

'This is my beloved Son; listen to him.'

Then Jesus led them down from the mountain, away from this exalted experience, into the hubbub of a noisy multitude thronging round a boy suffering from epileptic fits.

'Can you help us?' pleaded the boy's father. 'The boy has been like this ever since he was a baby.'

'All things are possible,' said Jesus, 'to the man who believes.'

Immediately the boy's father cried out, 'I believe; help my unbelief.' At that word, Jesus commanded the 'spirit' within the boy to come out and leave him. The boy fell into a fit that left him lying on the ground as if he were dead, but Jesus took him by the hand and lifted him up, and gave him back in good health to his father.

When they were alone with Jesus, his disciples asked him, 'Why could we not heal that boy? We tried to do it but failed.'

'Healing of this kind,' said Jesus, 'cannot be done except by prayer.'

Time was moving on for Jesus and his friends round the lake. Jesus was approaching a decisive moment of his life. Was he to stay in Galilee, or was he to make his mission known in Jerusalem? News about him had already reached the capital city, and some of the Jewish religious leaders had been in Galilee to see him and hear him.

But the heart of Jesus was still concentrated on his disciples. From Galilee to the Mount of Transfiguration, step by step, he had walked with his disciples. He had shown them his power in miracles of healing, in the stilling of the tempest, in providing food for hungry thousands. He had taught them how to pray and had given them a model prayer to follow. He had taught them to think of God as his Father.

Now he decided he must move with them to Jerusalem so that they might see even more deeply into the inner meaning of his life—and death. He began to speak to them about the end of his life; that he would be killed, and on the third day rise again. This was something they found it hard to understand and Peter blurted out,

'God forbid, Lord; this shall never happen to you!'—A hasty protest that brought a stern rebuke from Jesus.

But the hasty, quick-tempered Peter had looked deeply into the heart of Jesus. This rough fisherman from the Galilean shore had been constantly in Christ's presence since the day he gave up his calling to follow him. He watched him at work and his heart was stirred by what he saw. But most of all, captivated by Jesus, Peter's love went out to Jesus, and Jesus himself returned the affection and loyalty which Peter gave to him.

It all came to a climax one day at Caesarea Philippi in the country across the lake from Peter's home at Capernaum. There Jesus put the question to his men,

'Who do you say that I am?'

Peter was quick with the answer,

'You are the Christ, the Son of the living God.'

In that sentence Peter clinched the meaning of all the days of Jesus in Galilee. In the sunshine by the lake and on the hillsides round he had heard the greatest news of all time. Peter, the Galilean fisherman, had seen Christ, the Son of the living God, living on the soil of Galilee.

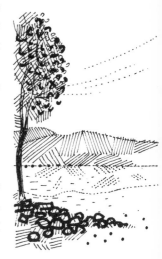

Out of the sunshine of Galilee—

—Jesus took the long, hard road to Jerusalem.

For Jesus and his disciples it meant the beginning of the road to Jerusalem. With the secret of the great confession in their hearts, they set out with Jesus on the road to the capital where their Master was to die and rise again. Some perhaps rebelled against this truth and hated the thought of it. But as they went up to Jerusalem they meditated on their Master's last words in Galilee—'he who loses his life for my sake will find it.' For them as well as Jesus the road to Jerusalem was the road to death—but also the road to life.

Matthew 10. 1–15, 12. 1–14, 13. 1–24,
16. 13–24, 17. 1–13; *Mark* 2. 1–12

17 PEOPLE ON THE ROAD

And they were on the road, going up to Jerusalem, and Jesus was walking ahead of them; and they were amazed, and those who followed were afraid. And taking the twelve again, he began to tell them what was to happen to him.

Mark 10. 32.

THERE WERE two main routes to Jerusalem from Galilee. The shorter one led through the land of Samaria, and the longer one down through the deep rift of the Jordan valley to Jericho, and then up to Jerusalem. It is likely that during his Galilee days Jesus may have gone up to the city by either one of these routes, but that he chose the Jordan route for his last visit to Jerusalem because it was a lonelier, less populated route. It gave him more time to be with his disciples, more time to think, and more time to prepare for the coming great events of his life.

How much more his disciples needed to learn from him was seen soon after they started from Galilee. James and John came to him with a very peculiar question.

'Master,' they said, 'we want you to do for us whatever we ask of you.'

'What is it?' asked Jesus.

'We want you to give us the right to sit, one at your right hand and one on your left, in your glory.'

Jesus was astonished at the request.

'You have asked something I cannot possibly give,' he said. 'You may suffer for my sake. You may go through all kinds of troubles and trials for my sake. You may even die for me, but to give you the position and authority you ask for is not mine to give.'

When the other ten disciples heard about this extraordinary request, they were indignant with James and John for putting themselves forward in such a manner. As

The river route led by way of Jericho.

they walked down the long, hot road beside the Jordan, the disciples grumbled among themselves, and stirred up hatred against James and John. Then Jesus called the twelve together and spoke to them clearly and firmly.

'You know,' he said, 'that the men of the world have people in high positions to govern them. They lord it over them to show how important they are. But it is different with you. As my disciples, if anyone would be great he must learn how to serve. He who would like to be first must be the servant of all. I am come among you not to be served but to serve and to give my own life for others.'

Jesus knew that as his mission moved towards its climax in Jerusalem, all kinds of people would like to join him as disciples. One man came up and said that he would follow Jesus wherever he went. Jesus looked at him and reminded him that even foxes have their holes to live in, and birds of the air have nests, but he had nowhere to lay his head. Was he prepared for this? Was he ready to be homeless for his Master's sake?

Another man, who looked to be a likely disciple, heard the call of Jesus. He was ready to join him, but he had an important excuse for not doing it at that moment. He had to bury his father. That must come first—and then he would follow Jesus. To him Jesus said, 'Leave the dead to bury their own dead; but as for you, go and proclaim the kingdom of God.' In other words there were plenty of people who could look after the funeral rites but the call to proclaim the kingdom was more important.

WHO IS MY NEIGHBOUR?

Another man said to Jesus, 'I will follow you, Lord, but let me first say good-bye to my family.'

'No,' said Jesus, 'you must put your hand to the plough and not look back. If you do, you are not fit for the kingdom of God.'

Jesus was looking for dedicated men. All the little excuses of life were very trivial indeed when compared with God's kingdom and its purposes. Jesus needed men who would go all out in his service.

Whenever Jesus stopped along the road, questioners came up to him. One man—a lawyer—put this question to him,

'What shall I do to inherit eternal life?'

'You know the law?' said Jesus.

'Yes,' said the lawyer, 'you shall love the Lord your God with all your heart, and with all your soul, with all your strength, and with all your mind—and your neighbour as yourself.'

'That's right,' said Jesus, 'do that and you will live.'

'But what about my neighbour?' asked the lawyer, 'Who is he?'

'Your neighbour?' asked Jesus.

'Listen. There was once a man going down the road from Jerusalem to Jericho—a lonely road and dangerous for travellers. He was set upon by robbers, stripped, beaten and left half-dead by the roadside. A priest came along, looked at him and passed by on the other side. Then a levite came along and he too passed the man by. But then came another traveller—a Samaritan who looked on the poor man, had pity on him, dressed his wounds with oil and wine, bound them up and took him to the nearest inn, and paid the bill in advance and offered to pay any extra charges.'

The lawyer listened to the story, and when Jesus asked him which of the men proved himself a real neighbour, he replied,

'The one who showed mercy on him.'

'Go thou and do likewise,' said Jesus.

Who is my real neighbour?

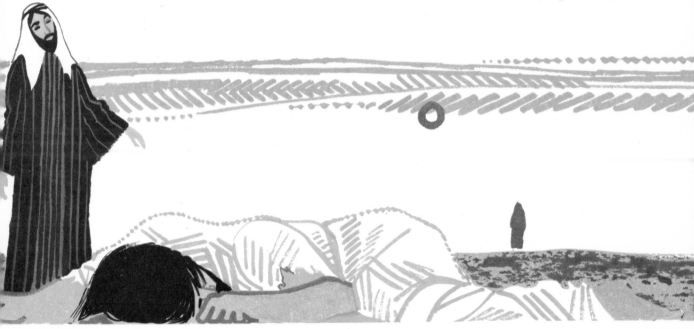

QUESTIONS AND QUESTIONERS

Jesus understood people. All along the road they came to him with questions and problems, but behind the questions was the questioner, whose question was usually put in order to hide himself behind it. Jesus looked behind all the words to the speaker himself. He was able to see inside a person's mind to the real question and the real person.

When a man came with the request that Jesus should divide up the family possessions between the man and his brother, Jesus immediately saw that the man was covetous. He turned to his disciples and warned them that life does not consist in having a lot of possessions, and he went on to tell them a parable.

'A rich farmer,' said Jesus, 'was prospering on his farm. His crops were bountiful, and his land was in good shape. In fact, he had no room to store all his crops. So he decided to pull down his old barns and build larger ones to store all his grain and his goods. One day the farmer said to himself that the time had come for him to take things easy. He had ample goods laid up for many years ahead, so he could eat, drink and be merry. That very night God said to him, "Your soul is required of you. Who is to have your possessions?"'

Anyone who lays up treasure for himself and is not rich towards God is missing the real meaning of life.

'Think of the birds of the heavens,' he said, 'they have neither storehouses nor barns and yet God feeds them. Think of the flowers in the fields, they neither toil nor spin and yet their beauty is more wonderful than anything Solomon could show. Do not worry about what you are to eat, or to drink, or how many clothes you have, for life is more important than food.'

'Some people,' said Jesus, 'lay up treasure in their houses, and along comes a thief and steals it. Some people keep their treasures and don't use them, so that the moth eats into them, or the rust destroys them. But you can have treasure which is never destroyed. Set your heart on the treasures of God and you will never need purses to keep it in—for your treasure is where your heart is.'

Every parable and story of Jesus was so true to life that the people he described came alive as he spoke, and the people who heard him easily remembered the point of the story.

One coin missing!

'A woman,' Jesus said, 'had ten silver coins. Every coin was precious. She kept them securely, but one day instead of ten coins there were only nine. Immediately she set to work to find the missing coin. She lit all the lamps in the house. She swept the house all through and looked into every corner. She was not happy until she found the coin, and then, to show her pleasure, she gave a party to celebrate the occasion.'

'Come and rejoice with me,' she said, 'for I have found the coin that was missing.'

'God is like that with people,' said Jesus. 'There is joy before the angels of God over one sinner who repents. Listen to this story.'

THE TWO BROTHERS

'A father once had two sons. They both lived at home happily in their father's house, helping on the farm. But one day the younger son came to his father and asked him for his share of the property. He wanted to leave home and go abroad. He wished to see the world and enjoy himself.

'The father agreed to share the property between his two sons and within a few days off went the younger son to a distant country. With money in his pocket he soon made friends and enjoyed himself spending freely in eating and drinking. But then the trouble began. His money was soon gone, and when a famine arose in the country he had no resources to fall back on. He went hungry and homeless, and was soon in real need. As a last hope he took on the job of looking after a farmer's pigs, and he was so hungry that he would gladly have eaten the food given to the pigs.

'In his misery,' said Jesus, 'the young man began to think. He knew that the hired servants of his father at home were better off than he was. They had food, clothing, and shelter, and he was perishing with hunger. I will go home, he decided, and ask my father to treat me as one of the servants and not as his son.

'All this time the father had been hoping that his son would come home again and often went out on the road expecting to see him coming. When he came, the father rushed to embrace him and ordered the servants to dress him in the best robe, with new shoes and a ring for his finger. A well-fatted calf was killed and a feast prepared to welcome home the lost son.

'"My son was dead," cried the father, "and here he is alive again: he was lost and is found."

'All the household were in the midst of a happy party when in came the elder brother. He had been working in the fields all day and was surprised to hear music and dancing.

'"It's your brother," the servants said, "he's come home again and your father has killed a calf to celebrate and we are all having a merry time."

'Your brother has come home. Let us have a party.'

'The elder brother was angry at the news, and refused to go into the party. When his father came out to beg him to come in, he pointed out that he had always obeyed his father, always stayed at home and worked hard on the farm. But never once did he get a party or a feast. But this brother, who had wasted the family money and lived a degraded life in a foreign country, was welcomed home with all this enthusiasm. It wasn't fair.

'His father pleaded with him. "Son," he said, "you are always with me, and all that is mine is yours. But this is your brother. He's come home again. We had lost him from our family, but now we have him again. Surely we ought all to be glad that he is with us again and our family circle is complete."'

For the father loved both his sons equally. Both sons were selfish and greedy, but their father's love never ceased and never wavered. He wanted both of them to be happy within his fatherly home.

TO SEE JESUS

It was in Jericho itself that the crowds were greatest. Deep down in the Jordan valley not far from the Dead Sea, Jericho attracted all sorts of people. Some came to Jericho for holidays, others for business. Jericho always seemed full of visitors. So the news that Jesus of Nazareth was coming into the town brought out a big crowd.

One man in particular was eager to get a sight of Jesus. He was a little man, called Zacchaeus, who belonged to the hated company of tax-collectors. Indeed Zacchaeus was a chief among the collectors and was said to have become very rich out of the money he got from his illegal methods of tax-collecting.

To get a good look at Jesus, Zacchaeus climbed up into a sycamore tree. There Jesus saw him, and called him by name to come down and to give him hospitality at his house.

Zacchaeus was thrilled to have Jesus of Nazareth in his home. It made him change his way of life. He started to give half his income to the poor and, if he did defraud anyone, to restore it fourfold. Zacchaeus was showing the new life that Jesus preached about. Jesus called him a 'true son of Abraham'. It was to Abraham's descendants that Jesus most of all wished to speak as he came to their capital city of Jerusalem. Zacchaeus heralded his arrival.

Face to face with Jesus made Zacchaeus a new man.

This is the King of men!

THE ROYAL ENTRY

He decided to ride into Jerusalem on a donkey, which would fulfil the Jewish prophecy that one day a king would come to Zion riding on a donkey. This would show the people, too, that his kingdom rested not on military force, but on the hope of universal peace.

So on the great day of the royal entry of Jesus, the disciples brought him the donkey from a village near Bethany. The little animal was there waiting to be used as Jesus had said, and the excited disciples used their coats to make a comfortable saddle for Jesus. They began to shout, 'Blessed be the king who comes in the name of the Lord! Peace in heaven and glory in the highest.'

As the procession moved over the top of the Mount of Olives and Jerusalem came into sight, Jesus stopped the donkey and looked out over the view. Tears came into his eyes as he saw the city and began to wonder what its future would be.

Down the rocky slope of the Mount of Olives the procession moved, with the little sure-footed donkey picking out his steps. The disciples were soon joined by crowds from Jerusalem, who threw their coats into the roadway and waved leafy branches of trees to welcome Jesus.

'Hosanna,' they shouted, 'Blessed is he who comes in the name of the Lord. Blessed be the kingdom of our father David that is coming. Hosanna in the highest.'

Mingling with the crowd were the cautious and suspicious Pharisees who came up to Jesus as he sat on the donkey and warned him to rebuke the crowds. This extravagant and popular welcome was getting out of hand, but all that Jesus said to them was, 'If these people are silent, then the very stones on the road will cry out.'

The royal welcome went on across the valley and up to the gates of Jerusalem. Amid shouts and singing, Jesus entered the capital city of the Jews as their king of Peace and Goodwill. Jesus looked at the cheering crowds and wondered how long they would continue to cheer. Was he the kind of king they were looking for? Would they recognize him in a few days' time? The days of crisis were drawing near, both for Jesus and the Jewish people.

Matthew 8. 18–22, 21. 1–11; *Mark* 10. 35–44;
Luke 9. 57–62, 10. 25–37, 12. 13–21, 15. 8–32, 19. 1–10

101

18 PEOPLE IN THE CITY

And he was teaching daily in the temple. The chief priests and the scribes and the principal men of the people sought to destroy him; but they did not find anything they could do, for all the people hung upon his words.   *Luke 19. 47, 48.*

Men not money matter most of all.

ON his first day in Jerusalem, Jesus came into the Temple area of the city and had his first big surprise. He saw the outer court of the Temple crowded with a noisy company of traders. There were the pigeon-sellers who sold their birds to pilgrims who came to worship and needed pigeons as a sacrificial offering. There were those who sold sheep and oxen for the wealthy worshippers to buy. The pens of the animals made the Temple area like a farmyard. But worse still were the money-changers with their tables loaded with 'temple money', ready to be exchanged for the everyday Roman coinage which worshippers carried in their pockets and purses. Every Jew had to give at least a half-shekel (about thirty-five cents) each year to the Temple, and the money-changers made a good profit out of their money changing.

Jesus was angry at the sight of all this trading and bargaining.

'This is my Father's house,' he said, 'you are making it a trading house.'

Making a small whip of cords, Jesus began driving the traders out of the courtyard with the sheep and the oxen. He overturned the tables of the money-changers, and scattered their coins on the ground.

'Get out,' he cried, 'this house of God is a house of prayer for all people. You are making it a den of robbers.'

Jesus was angry, not only because the traders and money-changers were doing their business in the Temple area but because they had chosen the court of the Gentiles. This was the only court that non-Jews could enter. Its desecration was a denial of the truth that Israel should be 'a light to the Gentiles'.

WHOSE AUTHORITY

As they watched Jesus driving out the traders and the money-changers, the Chief Priest and the Temple authorities grew angry. By what authority did he do this? Who gave him the right to sweep the Temple clean? Who was this man who claimed to have such power?

There in the Temple courtyard the angry religious leaders quickly got together to discuss what they should do. Not only were they angry with what Jesus had done to the traders, but because it meant that they too lost money. For giving permission to trade in the courtyard, the Temple authorities were well paid.

Jesus was losing them money. Not only was he upsetting the teaching of the Jews, but he was now striking at the heart of the Temple itself. He must be got rid of quickly—but how?

The authorities knew that the people were captivated by Jesus, and the power he showed. They flocked round him whenever he appeared in the streets. This man from Galilee was no ordinary prophet or soothsayer. He spoke many things which the people knew to be true. The authorities were getting frightened at his popularity, for it might mean the overthrow of their position.

So from that time onwards, they plotted to destroy him. A network of rumours was spread round the city about Jesus and his friends, and various tricks were tried to catch him in saying something illegal. Wherever Jesus spoke to a crowd of people a spy would be on the alert to report what he said to the authorities.

'You have a duty to God and man!'

'Teacher,' they said, 'we know that you speak and teach rightly. You show no favours to anyone. You really do teach the way of God.'

Jesus knew that this kind of talk was only the preparation for the real question to come.

'Tell us,' they said, 'Is it lawful to give tribute to Caesar, or not?'

Jesus knew that this was a crafty question. As part of the Roman Empire, all Jews had to pay their taxes and to use Roman coinage, but devout Jews hated doing this. If Jesus could be tricked on this question, then he might be arrested by the Roman governor.

GOD AND CAESAR

'Show me a coin,' said Jesus. A silver penny (worth about seventeen cents) was handed up to him. Jesus held the coin in his hand and looked at it, while the crowd wondered what he would say in answer to the question.

'Whose likeness is this on the penny?' asked Jesus. The spies sent by the Chief Priests looked a little foolish at the question, for everybody knew the answer.

'The likeness is Caesar's,' they said.

'Whose inscription is on the coin?' he asked.

'Caesar's, of course,' they said.

These were such simple questions. Everybody knew the answers. Why did he ask them?

Then came the reason why.

'If these answers are true,' said Jesus, 'then give to Caesar the things that rightfully belong to him, and give to God the things that rightfully belong to him.'

They all fell silent as Jesus answered. They had failed to catch him in an illegal statement and Jesus had thrown back the question to them. Every man owed a duty

*Who is putting in the
most money—the rich
man or the poor
widow?*

to God and to the state. Every Jew had to recognize this, even though it meant living
in the pagan Roman Empire. God came first in man's loyalty, but there was also a
loyalty due to the state.

THE POOR WIDOW

It was while he was looking at the comings and goings in the Temple area that
another person caught the eye of Jesus. He noticed a poor woman coming very humbly
into the Temple courtyard. By the way she was dressed it was clear she was a widow.
All round her were the throngs of well-to-do rich people coming into the Temple to
give their offerings to the Temple treasury. She too had come for the same purpose,
and Jesus stood by the treasury chest to see what would happen.

The rich pilgrims came up to the chest with their silver money and were obviously
pleased to be seen putting their money into the chest. They had much to give—and
they gave generously.

But Jesus watched the poor widow. How much would she give? He noticed that in
her fingers she held two little copper coins—the tiniest of all coins—worth a quarter of

a cent altogether. They were the ones that only the very poorest people used and the widow had brought two of them to give to God in the Temple.

It was all the money she had, and yet out of her poverty she gave everything. Unlike the rich givers who gave out of their plenty and did not really notice how much they gave, the poor widow offered her all to God.

The eye of Jesus fell on many kinds of people during those days in Jerusalem. He saw the streets filled with people going about their business caring for little else than money making. He saw the religious leaders worrying about the exact keeping of the law. His disciples too, were concerned about the 'signs of the time' and what would come at the 'end of the ages'. They wondered what would happen to the Temple buildings themselves. Would they still stand, or would they fall down?

Jesus did not give exact answers to all these questions, but he gave his disciples one parable which summed up all his teaching about the future.

THE WEDDING PARTY

'The kingdom of heaven,' he said, 'is like a wedding party in which ten girls took part. They were all dressed and prepared to meet the bridegroom and to take him to the wedding feast. To light the pathway of the bridegroom on his way to the celebrations, each of the ten girls had a lamp.

'Five of the girls, the foolish ones,' said Jesus, 'forgot to take an extra supply of oil

Be always ready with oil in your lamps.

for their lamps. But the wise ones were fully equipped with oil and wicks, ready to receive the bridegroom.

'When all was ready the news came that the bridegroom was delayed, and as it was late at night the foolish and the wise girls went to sleep. But at midnight the cry arose that the bridegroom was coming and that the lamps should be lit to welcome him.

'The girls quickly got ready and out came their lamps, and the lamps of the wise ones who had properly prepared for the bridegroom's coming were soon shining brightly.

'The foolish ones then saw their mistake and began to look round for oil.

'"Give us some of your oil," they pleaded with the wise ones.

'"No," came the reply, "we cannot do that, because if we do, then there may not be enough for us and for you. Go to the nearest shops and buy some.

'While the foolish ones slipped off to the shops to get their oil, the bridegroom arrived and was greeted by the wise attendants and lighted into the marriage feast, and the door was shut.

'Then came the foolish ones in haste from the shops with their lamps filled, the wicks trimmed and the lights brightly burning.

'"Lord, lord, open to us," they cried, as they knocked on the door of the marriage feast. But from within came the reply:

'"Truly, I say to you, I do not know you."

'So the door of the celebrations was kept shut and only those who had properly prepared for it were admitted.

'Watch, therefore,' said Jesus to his disciples, 'for you know neither the day nor the hour when the Lord is coming.'

*'You are not far from
the Kingdom of God,'
said Jesus.*

THE FIRST COMMANDMENT

Although he criticized the Scribes and the Pharisees, he knew that there were many good men among them. They understood the law and the prophets and knew that the outward observance of the law was not the only thing that mattered.

One scribe came to him, sincerely asking him for guidance.

'Which commandment,' he asked Jesus, 'is the first of all?'

'The first commandment,' answered Jesus, 'is "Hear O Israel: the Lord our God, the Lord is one; and you shall love the Lord your God with all your heart, and with all your mind, and with all your strength."

'But there is a second commandment,' said Jesus, 'which says "You shall love your neighbour as yourself." There is no other commandment greater than these.'

Jesus looked intently at the scribe. He gazed into his eyes and saw there the look of sincerity and humility.

'You are right, Master,' said the scribe, 'you have truly said that he is one, and that there is no other but he; and to love him with all the heart and with all the understanding, and with all the strength, and to love one's neighbour as oneself, is much more than all whole burnt offerings and sacrifices.'

Jesus listened to him and saw that he answered wisely.

'You are not far from the kingdom of God,' said Jesus.

It was almost the final question put to him in Jerusalem. St Mark says, 'after that no one dared to ask him any questions.' Jesus had dealt with all kinds of people—the poor and the rich, the religious and the sinners. He had shown himself to be the friend of all men, and the people of Jerusalem had welcomed him as King and Messiah. But the forces of opposition were gathering ground. Jesus knew that his days in Jerusalem were numbered and that before long the people, who now were friendly to him, would turn against him, and those who had shouted, 'Hosanna', would shout, 'Crucify'.

Matthew 25. 1–13; Mark 11. 15–18, 12. 28–34;

Luke 20. 21–26, 21. 1–4

19 PEOPLE IN THE VILLAGE

He went out of the city to Bethany and
lodged there.   *Matthew 21. 17.*

FROM THE bustle and noise of Jerusalem, Jesus went away every evening, as the sun set, to Bethany, to the home of his friends Martha, Mary and Lazarus. Jesus found in their home the peace and quiet he needed at the end of a strenuous day. It was not far to Bethany—just two miles over the ridge of the Mount of Olives and a little way down the other side.

The two sisters and their brother lived in a simple cottage-home in Bethany. Every evening they made ready to receive Jesus as he came home tired after the long day of speaking to people in the city streets and arguing with the religious leaders. The simple living-room of the home was carefully swept and the sleeping mats aired, the water to wash the feet of the visitors was got ready, and the evening meal prepared.

AT HOME IN BETHANY

One evening Martha was specially distracted by the crowd of people who came into the little home. They pushed into the room at supper time, which meant that everyone had to be given some food and drink. Martha was kept busy rushing to and fro while Mary sat quietly listening to Jesus.

At last Martha got so tired that she burst out with a complaint to Jesus.

'Do you not care,' she said to Jesus, 'that my sister has left me to serve alone? Tell her to help me.'

Jesus looked at the flushed and angry Martha.

'Martha, Martha,' he said, 'you are troubled and anxious with all this housekeeping. You are doing many things. You are making a lot of people happy and comfortable. But remember that Mary has chosen best by listening to me. She is playing her part in making your home a happy and welcome place. Both of you are needed.'

There was one sadness in the Bethany home—Lazarus was a sick man and gradually grew worse and died. Jesus was away in the countryside round Jerusalem when he heard the news, but he at once changed his plans and hastened back to Bethany to comfort Martha and Mary.

At home in Bethany.

Jesus wept as he looked at the weeping women, and was deeply moved at the sad company of friends who were with them.

'Where have you laid Lazarus?' Jesus asked.

'Come and see,' they said.

Walking ahead with Mary, Jesus came to the rough cave in the rock where the body of Lazarus was lying. Against the mouth of the cave a huge stone had been raised to protect the body from interference.

'Take away the stone,' ordered Jesus. The men heaved the great stone aside and the mouth of the cave lay open. Jesus prayed to his Father, 'I thank thee that thou hast heard me. I know that thou hearest me always. But this prayer is on behalf of the people who are standing by me—that they may believe that thou didst send me.'

Then Jesus came close to the mouth of the cave and looking into the dark, rocky inside he cried with a loud voice,

'Lazarus, come out.'

To the amazement of the onlookers, the dead man arose in the dark cave and came out into the sunlight with his feet and hands still in the bandages wrapped round him when he died.

'Unbind him,' said Jesus, 'and let him go.'

The news of what had happened at the burying place of Lazarus soon flashed through all the countryside, far beyond Bethany itself. When the news reached the Jewish High Priest, Caiaphas, in Jerusalem, he called his advisers together to see how they could get rid of Jesus. This man, they said to themselves, is dangerous. If he goes on like this, the people will believe that he really is the Messiah, the Son of God. So they plotted more determinedly than ever before to put Jesus to death.

IN SIMON'S HOME

One other home in Bethany besides that of Martha, Mary and Lazarus, was always open to Jesus. It was the home of Simon, the leper. It may be that Simon was related to Martha and Mary, and it is likely that Simon had been cured of his leprosy by Jesus. Jesus and his disciples were always welcome there.

One evening a supper party was arranged there for Jesus, as a farewell before he went again into Jerusalem. Jesus himself knew that he was coming to the time of decision in Jerusalem. The authorities had decided to put an end to his power among the people. But they were frightened of doing so at the time of the coming feast of the Passover, when Jerusalem would be full of people from all parts of the country.

As they sat at table for supper, Mary saw the opportunity she had been waiting for— the moment when she could show her deep love for Jesus. She had secretly purchased a pound of costly ointment made from the fragrant spikenard plant. The ointment

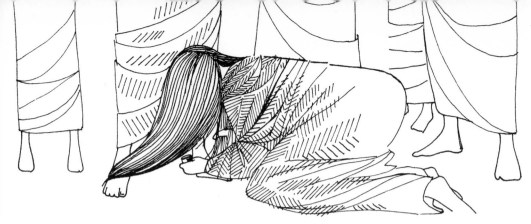

*What Mary did will
always be remembered.*

came all the way from India and was valued among the Jewish people as a fragrant perfume to be used only on special occasions.

Then Mary's moment came. Quickly and quietly, before any disciple could stop her, Mary knelt before Jesus, broke the box, poured out the ointment and swept her long hair across the feet of Jesus.

The fragrant smell of the ointment filled the house, and the amazed disciples began to grumble among themselves against Mary.

'Look, Master,' said Judas, 'Ought not this ointment to have been sold and given to the poor?'

Jesus looked at Judas and knew his love of money and how little he really cared for the poor. He looked round, too, at all his disciples and knew how little they realized what Mary had done for him.

'Why do you bother the woman?' he asked. 'She has done a beautiful thing to me. You have the poor always with you, but you will not always have me. Mary has done something to prepare me for my burial. She has anointed my body.'

'Truly I say to you,' Jesus went on, 'wherever the Gospel is preached in the whole world, what Mary has done will always be remembered.'

JUDAS'S BARGAIN

As soon as Jesus was safely in the home of Martha, Mary and Lazarus for the night, Judas Iscariot slipped out of the village, over the Mount of Olives and into Jerusalem. His secret mission was to the chief priests.

'What will you give me,' he asked, 'if I deliver Jesus to you? He is now in Bethany and is planning to enter Jerusalem as the hero of the people. Now is the time to act. How much will you give me?'

The chief priests looked into the eyes of Judas and saw there what Jesus had seen—the love of money.

'How much?' he asked, 'How much?'

The bargain was struck for thirty pieces of silver. Judas was satisfied. The chief

*'Are you the Christ,
the Son of God?'*

priests were satisfied too, because they had secured a betrayal inside the inner group of Jesus's disciples. They had taken a step that could lead to the death of this man who said that he was the Messiah and the Son of God. Such blasphemy was worthy of death. It was worth far more than thirty pieces of silver to make an end of Jesus of Nazareth.

Mark 14. 3–9, 14. 10–11; *Luke* 10. 38–41; *John* 11. 38–44

20 PEOPLE OF THE CROSS

So they took Jesus, and he went out, bearing his own cross, to the place called the place of a skull, which is called in Hebrew Golgotha. There they crucified him, and with him two others, one on either side, and Jesus between them. Pilate also wrote a title and put it on the cross; it read, 'Jesus of Nazareth, the King of the Jews.' *John* 19. 17–19.

'TELL US. Are you the Christ, the Son of God?' asked Caiaphas, the High Priest. Jesus stood before him in the hall of the palace in Jerusalem while the crowd of onlookers pushed in at the doorway. The glare of the torches lit up the scene as Caiaphas the Jewish leader questioned Jesus.

Jesus was silent. He looked at the bearded face of the High Priest and saw there the marks of anger and hatred. Caiaphas had plotted to arrest him and that night had succeeded.

'Have you no answer to make?' he said to Jesus. Caiaphas looked at this man whose message and methods so stirred the Jewish people. He had now got him in his power. From the Mount of Olives his men brought Jesus through the night into Jerusalem. With the help of Judas Iscariot and thirty pieces of silver, Caiaphas had triumphed over the man whose teaching shook the very foundations of Jewish life.

ARE YOU THE CHRIST?

'What do you say to these witnesses who accuse you?' Caiaphas said. But still Jesus was silent. Caiaphas was not used to such silence. In his High Priest's council men talked and argued, and if a man was accused he was usually eager to defend himself. But here was this silent Jesus of Nazareth. How could he get him to talk?

Caiaphas at last turned in anger to the silent Jesus.

'I order you by the living God to tell us if you are the Christ the Son of God.'

Then Jesus spoke, and Caiaphas lent eagerly forward to catch every word, for Jesus spoke quietly.

'You have said so,' replied Jesus. 'You will see the Son of Man seated at the right hand of power, and coming on the clouds of heaven.'

That was the word that Caiaphas was waiting for. At last he heard with his own ears the claim of Jesus to be the Christ.

'We do not need any more witnesses,' he cried to the assembled council, 'We have heard this blasphemy. What is your judgment?'

'Death!' they shouted, 'he deserves to be put to death.'

The news comes to Pilate.

Caiaphas and his council had no authority to put Jesus to death. They knew that the death sentence on Jesus must be passed under Roman law by the Roman governor—Pontius Pilate. So as the dawn broke over Jerusalem a messenger hastened across the city to the palace of the governor to warn Pilate that Jesus of Nazareth—now a prisoner of the Jews—was to be brought before him.

PILATE AND JESUS

Pilate had heard of this Jesus. He knew how troubled the High Priest was at what Jesus was doing among the people. But for Pilate it was just one more awkward and tiresome problem of these difficult Jewish people. He was not eager to see this Jesus who seemed to have done a lot of good wherever he went. Let the Jews deal with him themselves, he thought.

'Are you the king of the Jews?' he asked Jesus.

'You have said so,' replied Jesus.

Pilate wondered at this quiet reply of Jesus. All round him the Jews were hurling accusations, anxious to impress the governor, but Jesus gave no answer.

'Do you not hear these charges?' he asked Jesus.

Never before had Pilate met so strange a prisoner, who seemed to have done no wrong and committed no crime.

'Let him be crucified. Crucify him, crucify him!' The mob chanted the dread words. Pilate saw the cruel hatred in their faces as they shouted aloud for the death of Jesus.

'But why crucify him?' asked Pilate, 'What evil has he done? I can find no fault in him. I will scourge him and let him go.'

'Away with him! Crucify him!' they cried. 'If you release this man you are not a friend of the emperor. Everyone who makes himself a king sets himself against the emperor.'

The road to Calvary.

Pilate was startled at those words. If he released Jesus he would not only enrage the Jews but he might displease the emperor too. At last Pilate gave way. It was not worth risking a riot in Jerusalem. So he took a basin of water and in front of the crowd washed his hands and said to them,

'I am innocent of this man's blood; see to it yourselves.' Then he ordered Jesus to be taken away to be crucified.

The heavy wooden cross was laid across his shoulders and Jesus staggered under its weight. The hot afternoon sun poured down on him and the suffering he had already endured made the cross seem twice as heavy. The sympathetic Roman centurion in charge of the procession noticed that Jesus was fainting under the weight, and looked round for someone to carry the cross.

The centurion's eye fell on a strange face in the crowd. It may have been the eager look on the dark face that attracted his attention. He may have been just the first man the centurion's soldiers could grab among the spectators. It may have been that the man with the dark face was sorry for Jesus and came willingly to help him.

All we know is that Simon from Cyrene in North Africa was 'compelled'—according to the Gospel story—to carry the heavy cross, from which Jesus was to hang. It is likely that Simon was a Greek-speaking Jew on a visit to Jerusalem from his African home. His eagerness to see the sights of Jerusalem and to be near what was going on brought him out that afternoon into the streets. Just a visitor, perhaps, to Jerusalem, Simon of Cyrene stepped into the procession to help Jesus, and his name will never be forgotten.

*The centurion watched
—while his soldiers
played their game.*

THE MEN OF GOLGOTHA

On the summit of the mount of Golgotha, outside the city walls, people gathered to see the end of Jesus of Nazareth. They were a mixed group—the Roman centurion and his men, Simon of Cyrene, representatives of the High Priest, curious onlookers from the city mob who had followed the procession, and three women, including Mary, the mother of Jesus. Secretly, and in much fear of the mob, the women followed Jesus to the last, suffering moments of his life. They remained with him to the end.

But there were two other men at the cross of Jesus that afternoon—two men who had never been with Jesus before. This was their first and only meeting with him. Like Jesus, they too were hanging on crosses—one on each side of him. They were two thieves who, caught in the act of their thieving, had been condemned to die by crucifixion.

'Are you not the Christ?' said one of them to Jesus, 'If you are, save yourself and us from this torture.' He gasped out the words as he hung there in agony and misery.

But his companion on the third cross said to him, 'We are being punished for our misdeeds. But this man has done nothing wrong. Jesus, remember me when you come into your kingdom.'

Jesus replied to him, 'Truly you shall be with me in paradise.'

As the hours wore on the crowd on Calvary drifted away back into Jerusalem. Crucified criminals always took a long time dying and there was a thunderstorm blowing up. But one man, the Roman centurion, had to stay by the cross. He had to watch to the end the slow agonies of the crucified. His eyes were constantly fixed on Jesus. The centurion's men played a game of dice to pass the time away, and they auctioned the clothes of the crucified men. But the centurion himself could not take his eyes away from the figure of Jesus on his cross. Something about him held his attention. He had been present at many crucifixions and had seen many men die, but this Jesus of Nazareth was like no one he had ever seen.

'This man is truly God's Son,' said the centurion.

'Surely,' said the centurion to himself, 'this man is innocent.'

Gazing at Jesus the centurion looked in wonder at his patient, suffering face. The sky darkened, the thunder clouds gathered and the place shook with an earth tremor, but Jesus hung there in silent endurance.

Then suddenly the centurion saw Jesus lift his head and his strong clear voice rang out,

'Father, into thy hands I commit my spirit.'

One of the soldiers ran to give him a soothing drink, but the centurion saw that this cry of Jesus was the cry of a dying man. He had spoken his last word to God, and the Roman centurion fell silent.

'Surely,' he said to himself again, 'this man is not only innocent but he truly is the Son of God.'

PILATE'S VISITOR

Early that evening, Pontius Pilate had a visitor, a rich, well-known Jew.

All day Pilate had been worried about Jesus. Had he done right to condemn him? Ought he not to have resisted the Jewish High Priest and the Jewish mob? Pilate's wife, too, was worried with a secret fear that her husband had condemned an innocent man.

When Joseph of Arimathea came to ask for the body of Jesus to bury it in proper fashion, Pilate was surprised to know that Jesus was already dead. He sent for the centurion to check the facts and when he heard the news that Jesus was dead, he granted Joseph the privilege of burying the body.

So that night, as the sun set, Joseph of Arimathea laid Jesus in his own new tomb in a garden, and had a great stone heaved to the entrance, and the Jewish authorities were satisfied that all was secure. From the burying-place in the garden, the two Marys who had watched the crucifixion went sadly away. They had seen where he lay. But would he, could he rise again?

Matthew 26. 62–68, 27. 11–54; Mark 15. 33–47; Luke 23. 39–43

The tomb was sealed with a great rock.

21 PEOPLE OF THE RESURRECTION

But on the first day of the week, at early dawn, they went to the tomb, taking the spices which they had prepared. And they found the stone rolled away from the tomb, but when they went in they did not find the body. While they were perplexed about this, behold, two men stood by them in dazzling apparel; and as they were frightened and bowed their faces to the ground, the men said to them, 'Why do you seek the living among the dead?'   *Luke 24. 1–5.*

As the early light of dawn broke over Jerusalem three women crept silently out of the city towards the garden where the body of Jesus lay. In the crisp morning air they walked quickly with their cloaks wrapped closely round them. They were Mary Magdalene, Mary the mother of the disciple James, and Salome—all friends of Jesus who had cared for him and watched over him in his last dying moments. Underneath their cloaks they carried packets of fragrant spices to anoint his body as it lay in the tomb.

117

The women hastened through the silent streets of the city as they were anxious to be in the garden before anyone else could get there. All day on the Saturday they had been secretly preparing for this Sunday morning venture. It was the last act of their love for Jesus, and the women were frightened lest something should go wrong with their plans.

They had one big worry. Who would roll away the big stone which closed the mouth of the cave where Jesus lay? They had watched the men heave the stone into position and it would take strong men to move it again. How could three weak women move that rock?

They hurried on, believing that somehow they would be able to get into the cave to anoint the body of Jesus.

As they came near the garden the misty morning sky grew lighter but the garden itself was still in shadow. All was quiet. The women came in past the olive trees looking about for someone who might help them. Where was the guard the High Priest had ordered? There was no one about. How were they to get into the cave?

The rock had been rolled away. Then suddenly they saw that the mouth of the cave was open. The dark entrance was unguarded, the stone had been pushed aside. Someone had done what they were hoping for. In the morning half light, the women crept forward to the entrance trembling with suppressed excitement.

THE WOMEN AT THE TOMB

Step by step, they moved into the mouth of the cave. Their eyes strained into the interior, looking for the figure of Jesus lying there in the darkness. Suddenly they halted, transfixed to the ground. The figure of a young man rose to meet them, dressed in a white robe. Fear and terror clutched at their hearts as, in the gloom of the cave, he came towards them.

'Do not be frightened,' said the young man. 'You seek Jesus of Nazareth who was crucified. He has risen, he is not here. This is the place where they laid him.'

The cold, morning air drifted into the tomb as the women listened to the young man's voice. They were unable to speak. Fear struck them dumb. Turning out of the dark into the morning light they began to run.

'Go,' said the young man, 'go, tell his disciples and Peter that he is going before you to Galilee; there you will see him, as he told you.'

Fear and excitement impelled the women to run. Jesus was risen! All that he said had come true! The excited women hastened through the narrow streets to the house where the disciples were living. There, they told their story to the amazed company, who could hardly believe their ears. Was the women's story true? What had these frightened women seen there in the garden in the early dawn? Most of the disciples thought it was just an idle tale and did not believe them.

But as Peter listened to the women's story he decided there was only one way of testing its truth. He must go to the tomb and see for himself. So with another disciple Peter went up through the city streets to the garden outside the walls. It was now long past early morning. The sun was shining and Peter was certain that he did not see any strange figures in the garden. He looked round and made straight for the open tomb. The great stone had been moved. There was no doubt about that. Looking inside all that Peter could see were some linen cloths lying on the ledge of rock where Jesus had been laid. He was not there. He was gone, but where was he? Peter's heart was strangely moved as he walked silently away to tell his friends. Jesus was risen! The great truth sank slowly into Peter's heart.

The stranger on the road.

THE MEN ON THE ROAD

The same day two of the disciples set out to walk to Emmaus, a village seven miles across the hills from Jerusalem. The two men were glad to be out of the crowded, excited atmosphere of the city. They breathed the clean fresh air of the hills and were thankful to be together on the road. They planned to arrive at Emmaus by evening and to have supper there.

As they walked they talked about the events of the last week in Jerusalem. Every event of the week was fresh in their memories. It was all so memorable to them—the arrest of Jesus, his betrayal by Judas, the scene at the High Priest's house, the trial before Pilate, the crucifixion and the burial. They went sadly over each event, wondering whether the tragic end of their leader could have been avoided. They talked about him—his friendship, his way with his disciples, his deep sympathy and love.

Then they fell silent and walked on together while each of them pondered in his heart and wondered whether this was the end of Jesus and his teaching. They knew he was dead and buried—and yet they had heard that morning the strange tale of the women that the tomb had been found empty. Where was Jesus? Could it be that he was alive again?

As they wondered a stranger caught up with them on the road. He came up to them quietly, almost unnoticed, and walked along with them.

119

'You seem deep in thought,' the stranger said. 'May I ask what you have been talking about?'

The two men stood still and looked at the stranger. They were astonished that someone who had also come from Jerusalem should not guess what they had been talking about. They looked sadly at the stranger with downcast faces.

'Do you not know what has been happening in Jerusalem?' they asked.

'What has been happening?' the stranger asked.

'Why—the death of Jesus of Nazareth—this prophet, who we all hoped would be

'Stay with us to supper.'

the one to redeem Israel, has been put to death by crucifixion. Did you not know?'

They looked at the stranger in bewilderment.

'This Jesus whom we loved is dead—and yet this morning we heard the strange story that he was alive again—and that the tomb where he was buried is empty.'

Then the stranger began to talk with them as they walked on together to Emmaus. There was something about him which compelled them to listen closely. He walked between them with strong, steady strides along the dusty road.

'Don't you know,' he said, 'that all that has been happening in Jerusalem was prophesied about Christ? What you have seen and heard in Jerusalem was foretold in the Scriptures.'

The two men looked eagerly at the stranger. He seemed to know more than they did. His voice too had authority. They listened to his explanation of the Scriptures beginning with Moses. He showed them why Christ suffered and as he spoke their hearts were stirred for he seemed to speak like Jesus himself.

As they came near to Emmaus, the stranger said that he was going farther on, and would leave them in the village.

'Don't leave us,' they said, 'stay with us here. It is now nearly evening. Stay with us to supper, so that we can eat as well as talk together.'

So they came into the house at Emmaus where the table was spread for supper. They sat down at the table with the stranger, still wondering who he was and what his name might be. They watched him as he sat there at the table almost as their host instead of their guest. They saw his hands go out to take the bread and the way he held the bread was strangely familiar. He blessed the bread. He broke it and handed them each a piece—and then in a flash they knew. It was Jesus himself, and at that moment of recognition the stranger was gone.

They sat in amazement at the table.

They hurried back to Jerusalem.

'Did not our hearts burn within us as he talked to us along the road?' they said. 'Did we not hear him speak about the Scriptures? We ought to have known that it was Jesus.'

Without waiting any longer in Emmaus the two disciples returned to Jerusalem with their news. In the gathering darkness they hurried down the road so that the disciples in Jerusalem should know that night that Jesus was indeed risen from the dead. The seven miles to Jerusalem seemed long, long miles to the two men who were eager to tell the good news to the disciples.

JESUS APPEARS

At last they got to Jerusalem in the dark and found the disciples gathered excitedly round Simon Peter. As they entered the room Peter was telling his friends how he had

found the tomb empty. Everyone turned to greet the newcomers whose radiant faces showed that they too had great, good news.

'The Lord has risen and has appeared to Simon,' cried the disciples. 'What is your news?'

Then they told the story of their encounter on the road to Emmaus, and how Jesus was made known to them as he broke the bread at the table. They were sure it was Jesus. Some still doubted and wondered whether the excited men from Emmaus had not been deceived by a passing stranger who seemed to have the same face and figure as Jesus.

They were now sure that the tomb was empty and that Jesus was not there. The women's story too had been confirmed by Peter—but what were they to make of the Emmaus story?

As they stood wondering they saw Jesus himself standing in the room.

'Why are you troubled?' he asked, 'Why do these questionings arise in your hearts? See my hands and my feet. Handle me and see. It is myself. Have you anything to eat?'

They gave Jesus a piece of broiled fish, and as they watched him eat it they knew that he was a real person and was alive again among them.

THOMAS DOUBTS

But some disciples still doubted. One of them was Thomas. When his fellow disciples came to him with the news that Jesus was alive he refused to believe.

'We have seen the Lord,' they said.

Thomas looked at his friends. How could they possibly believe this to be true? he thought to himself. They must have seen a spirit, or had a vision. He had seen Jesus dead on the cross. He knew that he had been nailed there and that his side had been pierced. He had seen him taken down from the cross and laid in the tomb. He knew that Jesus was crucified, dead and buried.

'No,' he said, 'I cannot believe it is true. Unless I see in his hands the print of the nails, and place my hand in his side, I will not believe.'

Eight days later the disciples were again together and Thomas was with them.

When the doors of the room were shut Jesus came and stood among them. He looked at Thomas, and then said to him,

'Thomas, put your finger here.'

Jesus held out both his hands to Thomas with the black and bruised holes where the nails had been driven in.

Thomas touched the hands of Jesus and pressed his finger to the nail marks.

'Put your hand here,' said Jesus pointing to his side, 'and feel the wound made by the spear.'

But Thomas doubted.

'Do not be faithless, Thomas, but believe.'

Thomas looked at Jesus, and knew that he had been faithless. He knew that this was Jesus, his Master. This was the Jesus he loved. At last all the doubts he had were thrown away and he cried aloud to Jesus, 'My Lord, and my God.'

'Yes, you have believed, Thomas,' said Jesus to him, 'because you have seen me. But there are many who have not seen me and yet believe. Blessed are those people for their faith.'

Mark 16. 1–8; *Luke* 24. 1–41; *John* 20. 24–29,

22 PEOPLE AT PENTECOST

And all who believed were together and had all things in common; and they sold their possessions and goods and distributed them to all, as any had need. And day by day, attending the temple together and breaking bread in their homes, they partook of food with glad and generous hearts, praising God and having favor with all the people. And the Lord added to their number day by day those who were being saved.

Acts 2. 44–47.

'You are to be my witnesses in every part of the world,' said Jesus to his disciples as they stood round him on the Mount of Olives. There, in the last few hours of his days on earth, Jesus gave his men their marching orders. He had risen from the dead. He was alive—but he depended on them to tell the world the good news about himself.

Coming down from the Mount of Olives, the disciples assembled in the upper room in Jerusalem where Jesus had often been with them. All the eleven disciples were there, and one of their first duties was to chose the twelfth disciple, in place of Judas Iscariot. They chose Matthias as one who also had seen Jesus after the resurrection, and could join with the whole company in telling people that Jesus had risen from the dead.

So there in the upper room they met to pray and to plan for the future. They included Peter, John, James, Andrew, Philip, Thomas, Bartholomew, Matthew,

James son of Alphaeus, Simon, and Judas son of James. With them were Mary Magdalene, Salome and Mary, the mother of Jesus. They had all lived through the experiences of the Crucifixion and Resurrection, and now that Jesus had gone from them they drew closely together as people of one heart and one mind.

To tell men about Jesus and the Resurrection! That was what they were eager to do more than anything else. The wonderful news that Jesus of Nazareth was none other than the Son of God, and that in him all the Scriptures were fulfilled! This was the good news they had to give to their own Jewish brethren and to all the rest of the world.

They had the promise of Jesus that the Holy Spirit would descend upon them and give them the power to preach, and that through the Holy Spirit they would be able to speak to men of all countries and languages.

So in the quiet upper room in Jerusalem the little group of praying men and women were waiting in hope and expectation. Outside, the streets of Jerusalem were thronged with visitors who had come from all parts of the Jewish world for the Feast of Pentecost —the time of celebration of the end of the barley harvest, when devout Jews brought freshly baked loaves of fine flour to the Temple.

PILGRIMS IN JERUSALEM

Pentecost was a time of homecoming for Jews who lived in the countries round the Mediterranean. From the far distant lands of Mesopotamia where the great rivers Euphrates and Tigris flowed; from Egypt and along the North African coast; from the island of Crete and the deserts of Arabia—they had come up to worship and to visit friends in Jerusalem.

They gathered in the upper room.

Many of them were naturally curious to know about what had happened to Jesus of Nazareth, and to hear the story that he had risen from the dead.

So when the day of Pentecost came, the disciples knew that their message about Jesus and the Resurrection would be eagerly listened to in Jerusalem. In the upper room they waited and prayed for the promise of Jesus to come true.

As they were all together that morning, there was a sudden sweeping sound, as if a mighty wind was rushing through the room. They were all caught up in the power of the great wind, and there appeared tongues of fire which rested on each one of them. The Holy Spirit of God came on them in great power so that every person in the room was charged with fresh energy and was renewed in his mind and spirit.

Under the power of the Holy Spirit, the little company of people from the upper room burst into the streets of Jerusalem with their message about Jesus of Nazareth. They quickly drew large crowds to hear them. People were astonished to hear this little group of Jews speaking in many different languages. How was it these rough, uneducated men could do this? How was it that people from so many different countries could hear and understand what they were saying? Were these people drunk? Were they mad?

These were the questions that the people in the streets of Jerusalem asked as the disciples spoke of Jesus and the Resurrection. Something quite new was happening in Jerusalem. The power of God was being seen and felt in a new way. How could it be explained?

Then Peter stood up in the street and lifted up his voice to speak.

'Men of Judea and all who are in Jerusalem, listen to me, and give ear to my words,' he said. 'These men you have been listening to are not drunk. They are not filled with new wine. These men have a message from God to all the Jewish people. Listen to me.

125

'This Jesus,' said Peter, 'who was crucified in Jerusalem, has been raised from the dead by God. We are witnesses of this fact. This Jesus is now with his Father, and today the Holy Spirit has been poured out upon us in Jerusalem. That is why we can speak like this. It is God speaking through us to you.,

IN THE NAME OF JESUS

The crowds knew that Peter was only a Galilean fisherman. But his flaming, eager speech showed him to be a leader. They watched his face alight with truth and conviction. They heard him expound the Scriptures in a new way. He showed how all that happened in Jewish history led to this man, Jesus of Nazareth, who was the Christ, the Son of God.

'What shall we do?' cried many of Peter's listeners.

'Repent and be baptized, every one of you, in the name of Jesus Christ, for the forgiveness of your sins. You will then receive the gift of the Holy Spirit,' replied Peter.

So great was the effect of his words and of the enthusiasm of the disciples that hundreds of people were baptized that day. By the end of the day of Pentecost, over three thousand people had joined the little group from the upper room, and were learning about Jesus and the Resurrection from the apostles.

Soon after the day of Pentecost, Peter and John were going into the Temple at the hour of prayer. At all the entrances to the Temple, beggars gathered to ask for alms. Seeing Peter and John, a lame man held out his hand for a gift.

'I have no silver and gold,' said Peter, 'but I will give you what I have. In the name of Jesus Christ of Nazareth, get up and walk.'

Peter took the lame man by the hand and raised him up. Immediately, his weak ankles were made strong and he was able to stand upright by himself. He leaped up and walked about the Temple area to show people how strong he was.

As the man walked along with Peter and John, a crowd followed them, amazed at what had happened to the lame man. At last Peter turned round and said to them,

*'In the name of Jesus
get up and walk.'*

'Men of Israel why do you wonder at what has happened to this man? Why do you stare at us? We did not make this man walk. It is faith in the name of Jesus Christ which has made this man strong again. This is the same Jesus who was crucified and who rose from the dead. This man is now in perfect health through faith in his name.'

News of the miracle in the Temple soon reached the ears of the High Priest, who had Peter and John arrested.

'By what power did you do this?' they were asked.

'In the name of Jesus Christ of Nazareth whom you crucified and whom God raised from the dead. By him this man is standing now before you.'

Finding no crime for which they could be punished, the High Priest released Peter and John, warning them not to do any more preaching in the name of Jesus of Nazareth.

'We must speak,' said Peter 'of what we have seen and heard. We must listen to God rather than to you.' Then they returned to the warm, intimate fellowship of the upper room where the disciples were eager to welcome their two leaders safe and sound.

Inside the group they shared everything—food, money, possessions. Everyone brought what he had and put it at the service of the whole group. No one was poor or hungry. No one was rich or had too many possessions. Those who had land sold it and put the money in the common purse. Everyone was provided for according to his needs.

THE HIGH PRIEST'S OPPOSITION

But outside the group, the storm of opposition was growing. Every time Peter and John walked through the streets to the Temple area, crowds followed them, and the chief priests grew angry when they saw how popular the two men were. They arrested them and put them in prison, but the same night the doors of the prison were miraculously opened and the two men walked out.

Again they were arrested and brought before the High Priest's council.

'We charged you not to teach in the name of Jesus of Nazareth.'

But Peter replied, 'This Jesus is the Son of God. We obey him.'

At this the council members were enraged and wanted to kill the two men.

But an old and wise council member, called Gamaliel, stood up and uttered a warning note to his fellow members.

'Take care,' he said, 'what you do with these men. Take a warning from the past. Other men have claimed wonderful things and their schemes have failed. So if these men are like the others they too will come to nothing. But it may be that this teaching about Jesus of Nazareth is true and that this group of men are under the power of God. If that is so then nothing you can do can stop it.'

So the council took Gamaliel's advice, and after Peter and John were beaten with rods they were released. Once more they were ordered not to speak in the name of Jesus of Nazareth. But every day in the Temple area the disciples disobeyed the order and never ceased teaching and preaching about Jesus as the Christ.

Still the storm grew, and the high priests were constantly on the watch to catch the disciples in speaking blasphemy, or making claims for Jesus of Nazareth which were contrary to Jewish law.

They appointed a young Jewish leader called Saul of Tarsus to be their special agent in watching over the activities of the followers of Jesus of Nazareth. An educated young man, Saul was well trained in Jewish law and customs. He knew the rules and regulations of the Jewish way of life and was eager to show his ability to those in authority. He not only carried out his orders but went far beyond them. He set out to persecute and destroy this fast-growing sect which regarded Jesus of Nazareth as their leader.

Saul's chance came when Stephen, a younger member of the upper room group and a 'deacon' who helped the apostles in the management of the affairs of the whole company, was arrested. Stephen, 'full of grace and power' was brought before the High Priest's council for speaking against the Jewish law and the Temple.

'Is this true?' the High Priest asked Stephen.

For answer, Stephen reminded the High Priest that all Jewish history pointed to the coming of a 'Righteous One' who would deliver the Jewish people from their sins and bring in the reign of God. From Abraham onwards, to Moses, and David, Stephen said that God's promise was of the 'Righteous One' who would come.

'You have now betrayed and murdered the Righteous One, who is Jesus of Nazareth,' cried Stephen.

At these words the council fell into a rage and ground their teeth at the young man.

But Stephen calmly said, 'Behold I saw the heavens open, and the Son of Man standing at the right hand of God.'

At this the whole council rose as one man, and stopped their ears in order not to hear any more blasphemies. They rushed Stephen out of the court and ordered him to be stoned to death.

SAUL AND STEPHEN

Saul was among those who shouted for Stephen's death, and as the men threw the stones Saul stood by watching, and looking after the clothes of the men who were doing the stoning.

As he died, Stephen cried aloud, 'Lord Jesus, receive my spirit.'

While the heavy stones rained on him, he prayed, 'Lord do not hold this sin against these people.'

Saul of Tarsus watched Stephen die. From that day he set afoot an intense persecution of the church in Jerusalem. He entered house after house and dragged out the followers of Jesus of Nazareth to prison and death. He was determined to rout out this false teaching in its place of origin.

But the preaching about Jesus of Nazareth never ceased. The good news went beyond Jerusalem, for the story of what had happened at Pentecost was carried home by the many pilgrims who had heard the news in their own tongues. The little group in the upper room continued in prayer and in sharing all their possessions.

The High Priest and his special agent, Saul of Tarsus were convinced that this Jesus of Nazareth teaching must be stopped. If it could not be stopped it would spread among all the Jewish people. To stop it spreading became the life commitment of Saul of Tarsus.

Acts 1. 12–14, 2. 1–14, 3. 1–10, 5. 34–40, 6. 8–15, 7. 54–60

23 PEOPLE OF THE NEW WAY

Now those who were scattered went about preaching the word. Philip went down to a city of Samaria, and proclaimed to them the Christ. And the multitudes with one accord gave heed to what was said by Philip, when they heard him and saw the signs which he did. For unclean spirits came out of many who were possessed, crying with a loud voice; and many who were paralyzed or lame were healed. So there was much joy in that city. *Acts* 8. 4–8.

Road through the desert.

THE LONG, hard road ran across the desert from Jerusalem to Gaza, leading on towards Egypt. It was a good, well-made road used by Roman troops and by the chariots of business men and pilgrims going to and from Jerusalem. The hot sun beat down on it, and travellers were always glad to move off the road into the shade of a tree.

Philip, the young deacon from the church in Jerusalem, stood by the roadside waiting and watching. His eyes strained up and down the road, hoping and expecting to see a traveller. He had come down to the Gaza road from Samaria in obedience to a heavenly vision which told him to keep watch on the desert road that led on to the south.

129

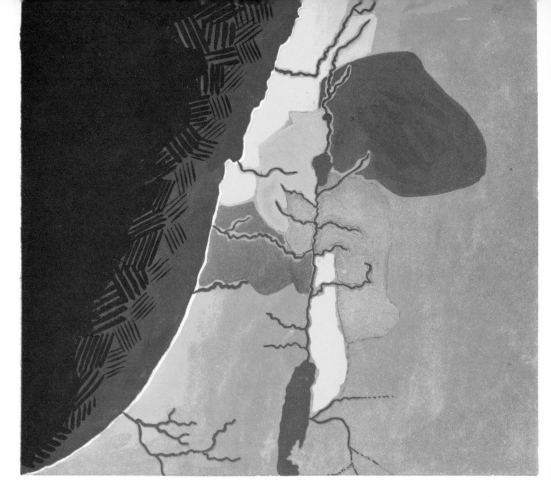

The land of Jesus lay between the desert and the sea.

As a young preacher from the church in Jerusalem, Philip was glad to be out on the roads of Palestine to tell people the good news about Jesus of Nazareth. The road from Jerusalem to Samaria had taken him into a foreign country where many people had been baptized. Now he was on another road which led on to Egypt and Africa, which also needed to hear the Gospel. Philip had already learned the great truth that the good news about Jesus was not only for the Jewish people but for people of every country.

RIDER IN THE CHARIOT

Philip's eye caught a distant cloud of dust far down the road towards Jerusalem. In the bright sunlight he looked eagerly towards it as the cloud gradually came nearer. Soon he could pick out the galloping horses and then a chariot. Philip moved out into the roadway and held up his hand. The chariot slowed down, the horses panting for breath as the charioteer reined them in.

Running up to the chariot, Philip saw a dark-skinned man sitting in the passenger seat reading a scroll. He seemed pleased to see Philip and asked him to come up and sit with him.

Philip looked at the man, and then at the scroll he was reading.

'Do you know what this scroll is?' asked Philip, 'Do you understand what you are reading?'

'How can I understand,' replied the traveller, 'unless someone guides me?'

'Who are you?' asked Philip.

'I am an Ethiopian—the finance minister of the Queen of the Ethiopians, and I am on my way home from Jerusalem, where I bought a copy of this scroll of Isaiah's prophecy. Look, what does this mean?'

With his finger the Ethiopian spelt out the words,

> As a sheep led to the slaughter
> or a lamb before its shearer is dumb
> so he opens not his mouth.
> In his humiliation justice was denied him.
> Who can describe his generation?
> For his life is taken up from the earth.

'Who is the writer referring to? Does he say this about himself; or about someone else?'

Then Philip saw his chance. As the chariot rolled on under the hot sun he started to tell his companion of the meaning of Isaiah's prophecy. He told him of the good news of Jesus of Nazareth in whose name he could be baptized and his sins forgiven.

The dark face of the Ethiopian traveller glowed with delight as Philip explained to him the secrets of the Scripture and how Jesus of Nazareth was the fulfilment of the hopes of the prophets.

Water in the desert!

'Look,' he said, as the chariot swept by a roadside pool, 'There is water. What prevents me from being baptized?'

The chariot was stopped and Philip and the Ethiopian got down and stepped into the water where Philip baptized him. As soon as they came out of the water the Spirit caught away Philip and the Ethiopian was left alone by the roadside. He climbed back into his chariot and drove on homewards a happy man.

THE DAMASCUS ROAD

On the high road from Jerusalem to Damascus, Saul of Tarsus had nearly reached the end of his journey. He was commissioned by the High Priest in Jerusalem to seek out any Jews in Damascus who believed in Jesus of Nazareth, and to bring them as prisoners to Jerusalem. He marched on down the road intent on his mission of persecution. In his pouch he carried his letters of authority from the High Priest, and with him were his assistants ready to spy out those Jews who had turned to following this Jesus of Nazareth. They hoped to capture many of them in Damascus.

As they came near Damascus, Saul urged his comrades to be ruthless in their searches. They were not to be afraid of anyone, and were to threaten with death those who blasphemed against God, and claimed that Jesus of Nazareth was God's son.

Suddenly, as Saul spoke, a bright light flashed across the road on to Saul's head and face. He fell to the ground with his hands shielding his face from the brilliant light. A voice spoke,

'Saul, Saul, why do you persecute me?'

'Who are you, Lord?' he replied.

'I am Jesus, whom you are persecuting. But rise, go on to Damascus and you will be told what to do.'

The men with him were speechless. They heard the voice speaking to Saul but saw no one. With his eyes still blinded by the flash of light Saul groped round with his hands, and his friends led him to a house in the city in the street called Straight, where for three days he rested, neither eating anything nor able to see.

After three days, a secret disciple in Damascus named Ananias was warned by God to visit Saul. But Ananias was afraid of doing so.

'Lord,' he said in his prayer, 'I have heard about this man. He is here to arrest any who call on the name of Jesus and to take them prisoner to Jerusalem.'

'Go, Ananias,' came the answer 'for this man Saul has now been chosen to carry the name of Jesus to all the people beyond Israel.'

So Ananias went down to the house in Straight Street, Damascus, and there laid his hands on Saul's head.

'Brother Saul,' he said, 'the Lord Jesus who came to you in the flash of light on the road has sent me to you to give you back your sight and to give you the power of the Holy Spirit.'

Saul's sight came back. He was baptized, ate food, and rose up a new man with the new name of Paul, ready to be an ambassador for the Jesus he had persecuted.

As soon as the Jews in Damascus saw what had happened to their leader from Jerusalem, they began to plot against him. But with fearless bravery Paul went into the synagogues of the city and proclaimed that this Jesus he had hated was the Son of God. He showed the congregations through their own Scriptures that this Jesus was none other than the Christ. This made them rise up in fury and prepare to kill him.

By day and night the Jews of Damascus watched the city gates so that Paul could not escape. They guarded the house where he lived and watched him in the streets. But in the darkness of the night Paul outwitted them by being let down over the wall of Damascus in a basket. When the dawn came, he was well on his way back to Jerusalem where he preached boldly in the name of Christ.

AT HOME IN JOPPA

The road to the sea from Jerusalem led to the little port of Joppa. The good news of Jesus travelled speedily down the road and a group of followers of Jesus soon grew up in Joppa. One of their leaders was Dorcas, who gave her time in the service of others. Expert with her needle, Dorcas made clothes for the poorer people of the Christian group in Joppa, and her kindness and generosity to her neighbours made her greatly beloved. Week by week, she gathered her friends together to make coats and garments of all kinds, especially for the widows who belonged to the Christian community.

'Dorcas, arise!'

Then, suddenly, Dorcas died, and the Joppa Christians were sad and very sorrowful. They sent the news to near-by Lydda where Peter was staying.

'Please come to us quickly,' they said, 'Dorcas is dead.'

So Peter came down the short stretch of road from Lydda to Joppa with a sad heart, because he loved and respected Dorcas for her faithful devotion. He determined that he would call on the power of God to raise Dorcas from the dead.

When he entered the house he put all the mourners outside and knelt down and prayed by the body of Dorcas. Then he turned to the body and cried in a loud voice, 'Dorcas, arise!'

As Peter watched, he saw Dorcas slowly open her eyes. Peter gave her his hand and lifted her up. Calling together all her friends, Peter presented Dorcas to them alive and well, and Peter stayed on in Joppa to rejoice with his friends.

The wonderful news of what Peter had done in Joppa spread through all the countryside. Travellers carried the news down the roads which ran along the sea-shore even as far as Caesarea—the headquarters of the Roman army. It was in Caesarea that Cornelius, a Roman centurion from Italy, lived—a man who had become a believer in Jesus of Nazareth. Like Dorcas, he was full of charitable works and gave money generously to the people.

One night, Cornelius had a vision of God which startled him.

133

'Cornelius,' said the voice, 'send messengers to Joppa to Peter the Apostle, who is living with Simon the Tanner in his house by the sea-side.'

Wondering what this could mean, Cornelius ordered two of his servants and a soldier from the guard to go down the road to Joppa and, if possible, to bring Peter to Caesarea. The men set off wondering what they would say to the apostle as a reason for their request. What could be the purpose of this message. But, like good servants, they obeyed their master Cornelius and came to the house of Simon the Tanner.

While the men were marching down the road to Joppa Peter himself had a strange preparation for their visit. He was on the flat roof of Simon's house at the noon hour of prayer when he fell into a trance and had a vision. He saw the heaven open, and a great sheet descended to him held up at its four corners. In it were all kinds of animals and birds of the air, and Peter heard a voice, 'Rise, Peter, kill and eat.'

Peter was hungry and the vision he saw tempted his appetite, but Peter was a good Jew and carefully observed the customs of his people.

'No, Lord, I cannot eat this kind of food. I have never eaten anything that is common or unclean.' The voice came a second time, 'What God calls clean, you must not call common.'

As the great sheet disappeared Peter woke from his dream, and almost immediately came the message that three men from Caesarea were asking for him and were waiting at the door.

'Go with them,' said the Spirit to Peter, 'Don't hesitate for I have sent them.'

Peter went down to the men and asked them why they had come.

'Cornelius, the centurion of Caesarea, sent us. He is a God-fearing man and well respected by all the Jewish people. He wants you to come to his house and to speak with you.'

The next day, Peter and other Christians from Joppa set off with the soldier and the

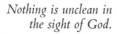

Nothing is unclean in the sight of God.

two servants for Caesarea, where the centurion was anxiously awaiting Peter's arrival. As soon as Peter entered his house, Cornelius knelt down at his feet and worshipped him. But Peter lifted him up with the words,

'Stand up; for I too am a man. God has been showing me that in his sight there is no difference between people. Every man of every nation who fears God and does what is right is acceptable to him. You a Roman, I a Jew, are brethren through Jesus Christ.'

As Peter spoke the Holy Spirit came on the whole company—Jews and Gentiles alike and they all praised God and were baptized by Peter in the name of Jesus Christ.

PETER IN PRISON

Soon after his meeting with Cornelius, the Roman centurion, Peter was arrested and put into prison by King Herod in Jerusalem as a precaution against popular disturbance.

Frightened by the power that Peter used, Herod chained him securely to two soldiers both by day and night, with sentries at the door to prevent his escape. In the middle of the night, as Peter slept in his chains, an angel of God awoke Peter. His chains fell off, the inner and outer gates of the prison flew back, and Peter found himself in the open street.

Wrapping his cloak round him, Peter hurried down the familiar streets to the house where he knew the disciples would be meeting. He was sure an angel of God had delivered him from prison, but how could he warn his friends that he really had escaped from prison? They might think it was a trick of King Herod's to throw them all into prison.

Hurrying down the dark street, Peter looked about him to see whether anyone was following him. All was quiet as he stopped before the house he knew so well. It was the home of Mary, the mother of the young man John Mark, Peter's friend, assistant and companion.

Peter came to the house he knew so well.

Peter knocked at the door of the gateway. He heard footsteps inside and immediately knew that it was Rhoda, the young maid who worked in John Mark's home.

'I am Peter,' he whispered. 'I have been delivered from prison. Let me in.'

Overcome with fear and joy, Rhoda, instead of opening the gate, ran back into the house to tell the disciples.

'Peter is at the gate,' she said. 'He's out of prison.'

'You are mad,' they shouted, 'it's his angel.'

'No,' said Rhoda 'I'm sure it's Peter. I know his voice so well. Hark, he is knocking.'

In the silence of the room they could hear the steady knock, knock, at the gateway.

'Let him in,' they all cried. Rhoda ran to the gate, opened it and there to the amazement and wonder of all the company was Peter safe and well once again.

135

They wanted to worship Paul and Barnabas.

One of the great roads of Palestine leads from Jerusalem to Antioch in the north, and in Antioch a strong Christian church quickly grew up. It was the home of Barnabas who brought the newly converted Paul there and introduced him to the Christian church. From Antioch, Barnabas and Paul went off on preaching tours together, and even crossed the sea to Cyprus.

On the island of Cyprus, the two men encountered the magician, Elymas, who was persuading people not to believe in the Christian teaching.

'You son of the evil one,' said Paul to him. 'You are an enemy of righteousness. You are full of deceit and evil. Now you will be blinded for a time and unable to see the sun.'

Immediately Elymas became blind, and for a time was unable to see the astonished wonderment of the people.

In the city of Lystra, on the mainland of Asia Minor, Paul and Barnabas gave new life to a cripple who had never been able to walk.

'Stand on your feet,' said Paul. The man sprang up and walked. When the crowd saw the miracle they shouted, 'The gods have come again, these two men are not men but gods. We must worship them.'

The citizens of Lystra began to bring oxen for sacrifice, and wanted to call Barnabas by the name of the god Zeus, and Paul they called Hermes. But Paul and Barnabas cried out,

'We are also men like you. Our message is that you should turn from idols to the worship of the living God, who is the God of all nations.'

With this message the two men marched along the Roman roads of Asia Minor. In some cities they were worshipped, and in some stoned and dragged out of the city. The Jews hated to hear them speak in the synagogues, and stirred up the crowds against them. But whatever happened, Paul and Barnabas never failed to preach that what God had done in Jesus of Nazareth was wonderful news for all men to hear and to obey. The words of Barnabas and Paul went home to the hearts of men and women of all kinds, of all races and languages. They showed the early Christians that the message of Jesus was indeed a message for all people.

Acts 8. 26–40, 9, 10, 12, 13

24 PEOPLE AT HOME

As they went on their way through the cities, they delivered to them for observance the decisions which had been reached by the apostles and elders who were at Jerusalem. So the churches were strengthened in the faith, and they increased in numbers daily.

Acts 16. 4–5.

THERE WAS great excitement in Timothy's home at Lystra. All round the house preparations were being made for visitors. News had come up from the south that Paul was on his way to Lystra and hoped to stay in Timothy's home. The news was very welcome to Eunice, Timothy's mother, and to his grandmother, Lois, for Paul was their friend. On his previous visit to Lystra, Paul had converted them to faith in Jesus Christ, and they in turn had instructed Timothy.

Timothy's father was a Greek and his mother a Jewess, a fact which made him doubly interesting to Paul. He had known the Old Treatment Scriptures from his youth and in Lystra he had come into touch with the thought of the young people of the city. Paul believed that Timothy could be of great help to him in explaining the truth of Jesus Christ both to Greeks and to Jews.

Paul knew how carefully and lovingly Eunice and Lois had watched over Timothy's upbringing. Their home was the meeting place of the Christians in Lystra. Here the little group of believers met for worship, and here all the people came who wanted to know more about 'the way' of Jesus of Nazareth.

In the midst of all this Timothy grew up, a loving son and grandson, devoted to the teachings which his family taught him. He too, was excited when he heard the news that Paul was coming to stay in their home, for he hoped that he might be able to go with Paul on his journeys.

Timothy goes with Paul and Silas.

Paul had Silas with him, chosen by the Christians in Antioch, as a travelling companion. The two men carried messages from Antioch to Lystra so that the Christians there might know what the Christians in Antioch were thinking and doing.

All the churches that Paul and Silas visited on their way to Lystra were small groups of people who usually met together in the homes of their members. Gathered in the family circle they cared for each other and were closely linked together in their loyalty to Jesus.

In Timothy's home the family regularly read the Scriptures and prayed together. His mother and grandmother were the leaders of the little 'church in the house' and Timothy himself was already called a 'disciple'. Far and wide over the area Christian people spoke well of him.

So, when Paul and Silas decided to take Timothy with them as companion and assistant, the Christians in Lystra were very happy. Paul referred to him as 'my true child in the faith' and 'my beloved child', and Paul and Silas and the elders of the church in Lystra 'laid their hands' upon him as a sign of his dedication to the Christian ministry.

'Come over the sea and help us.'

From that time onwards, Timothy travelled with Paul through the cities of Asia Minor, visiting the homes of the Christians, and, when he and Silas crossed into Europe, Timothy went with them.

'Come over and help us.' That was the cry that Paul heard in the night as he and Timothy and Silas were staying in the port of Troas, waiting for God's guidance.

'Come over and help us'—the cry came across the sea from Macedonia, the nearest part of Greece, and Paul could clearly see, in his vision, the figure of a man appealing to him to come. 'Come over and help us!'

The cry struck home to the heart of Paul and when he told Timothy and Silas about his vision all three men believed it was God's call to them to cross the sea to Greece.

It was the Sabbath day when Paul and his friends came down to the riverside at Philippi. They had heard that a number of women met on the river bank to pray and to think about the things of God. There in the warm sunshine Paul saw a number of women sitting on the river bank grouped round a woman who was clearly the leader.

Who was she? Paul discovered that her name was Lydia, a business-woman in the dyed goods trade. She came from Thyatira, a town famous for its dyes. Lydia's speciality was cloth dyed in purple, which she sold to the prosperous people of Philippi.

Paul and his friends sat down with the women and were soon in close conversation with them. Lydia in particular listened intently to what Paul had to say about Jesus of Nazareth, for she too worshipped God and her heart was open to Paul's teaching. She and all her household were baptized.

IN LYDIA'S HOME

'Come and live in our home,' said Lydia to Paul and Silas and Timothy. 'If I am judged to be faithful to Jesus of Nazareth, come and share our home.'

So the three men stayed in Lydia's home in Philippi enjoying the comfort and kindness which she provided for them, and from there they went out into the streets of the city preaching the good news of Jesus.

They were soon in trouble with the authorities for having cast out an evil spirit from a slave girl who was used by her owners to tell fortunes. When her owners saw that her powers of soothsaying had disappeared they dragged Paul and Silas to the magistrates.

'These Jews are disturbing the peace of our city,' they said. 'They are trying to teach fresh customs to the people, which are not for Roman citizens to follow.' The crowd attacked them, and the magistrates beat them with rods and threw them into the inner prison with their feet fastened in the stocks.

Suddenly, at midnight, as Paul and Silas were singing hymns and praying, there was an earthquake which opened all the doors of the prison and set every prisoner free. When the jailer saw what was happening he was afraid that all the prisoners would escape, which meant death for him. He was about to kill himself when Paul called out to him,

Set free by earthquake.

'We are all here. None have escaped. Don't harm yourself.'

The jailer was so astonished to see what had happened that he fell down on his knees in front of Paul and Silas crying,

'What must I do to be saved?'

'Believe in the Lord Jesus, all of you in this household,' said Paul.

At the dead of night the jailer took Paul and Silas into his home, washed the stripes from their beating, and was baptized with all his family. The next day when the magistrates heard what had happened in the prison, they told the police to let them go.

'No,' said Paul, 'let the magistrates themselves come to free us from prison. They beat us in public, although we are Roman citizens, and they did it without our being tried in a court of law.'

'Turning the world upside down,' they said.

When the magistrates heard that Paul and Silas were Roman citizens, they knew that they had acted illegally, so they came in haste to the prison and apologized to them, and asked them to leave the city quietly.

So Paul and Silas went home to Lydia's house, where the Christians in the city gathered together to meet them. There they stayed to rest and to talk with the brethren before they set out to visit Thessalonica.

From Lydia's home in Philippi, Paul, Silas and Timothy went on to Jason's home in Thessalonica. Jason, a respected citizen of Thessalonica was a Jew who had become a Christian, and it may be that he was related to Paul. In his friendly, hospitable home the three men rested and prepared to meet the Jews of the city. Paul's custom was to go to the Jewish synagogue and there by argument and reference to the Scriptures, try to show the Jews that Jesus of Nazareth was the fulfilment of all their hopes.

Many Jews in Thessalonica listened to Paul and Silas and were convinced by their teaching. Jason opened his house to all who wanted to talk privately to the visitors. Many Greeks came, and many of the leading women of the city, but most Jews remained unmoved. They were jealous of Paul and Silas and Timothy, until at last they stirred up a noisy rabble of men to attack Jason in his home. They dragged him out with Paul and Silas to the city magistrates.

'These men,' they said, 'are turning the world upside down. They did it in Philippi and now they've come here. This man Jason has received them into his home. It is all contrary to Roman law. These men say there is another king beside Caesar, a king called Jesus.'

As they listened to the story, the magistrates were troubled. They may have heard about what happened at Philippi. They knew that the men before them were not only Jews—but Roman citizens who could claim protection of the law. The men had done nothing illegal, nor had they created a disturbance. So they sent them home with Jason on Jason's guarantee that they would keep the peace.

Slipping away quietly from Thessalonica, Paul and his friends went southwards to Athens and Corinth. There in the synagogue he argued with the Jews, and in the market place he met the philosophers and thinkers of Athens.

'Who is this babbler?' they asked. 'He seems to talk about foreign gods, and about someone called Jesus who rose from the dead.'

Some of the philosophers got excited at these new ideas, and decided to give Paul a chance of speaking to them. So they brought him into the middle of the Areopagus where the judges and learned men met to discuss public questions.

'Men of Athens,' he said, 'I see many objects of worship in your city. You seem to be very religious. I saw one altar with the inscription *To the unknown God*. The God whom I worship is the God who made the world. He does not need shrines and altars made by human hands, for he gives life and breath to all things.'

The philosophers and thinkers of Athens listened to these confident words of Paul. Some of them smiled at his speech but others listened more intently.

'We are all God's children,' Paul went on, 'and there will come a day when he will judge the world in righteousness. He commands every man to repent of his sins. All this he has made clear by the One who has been raised from the dead.'

Many of his listeners mocked and laughed when he mentioned the resurrection from the dead, and others shook their heads and said, 'We will hear you again about this.'

THE TENT-MAKERS' HOME

From his encounter with the learned men of Athens, Paul went on to Corinth, to the home of Aquila and Priscilla. Driven out from Rome because they were Jews, Aquila and Priscilla had settled in Corinth to carry on their trade of tent-makers. There they joined the little company of believers in Jesus of Nazareth, and when Paul and his companions arrived from Athens, Aquila and Priscilla opened their home in welcome. Not only was Paul a fellow-Christian, but he was also a fellow tent-maker!

Tents for shepherds, and sails for sailors.

For eighteen months Aquila and Priscilla and Paul lived and worked together, sewing the skins of animals to be used in the country districts as tents for shepherds and tribesmen. They worked also on the sails needed for the ships that sailed in and out of Corinth. In this way, Paul earned enough money to keep himself and to be independent of any gifts from the churches.

But he regularly went to the synagogue in Corinth to preach and argue with his fellow Jews, many of whom believed in Paul's teaching and welcomed him, as well as Silas and Timothy, into their homes. Aquila and Priscilla became so attached to Paul that when he proposed to cross the sea again to Asia they offered to go with him, and to set up their home in Ephesus.

Another visitor was also entertained in their home in Ephesus. His name was Apollos—a Jew from Alexandria, whose eloquence attracted many people to hear him. He began to speak boldly in the synagogue but as they listened to him, Aquila and Priscilla realized that Apollos needed further guidance. So they took Apollos into their home and helped him to understand 'the way of God' more accurately. When the time came they wrote letters of introduction for Apollos to the churches in Greece.

While Paul was living with Aquila and Priscilla in Ephesus, a tremendous disturbance started in the city among the silversmiths of the city who lived by making silver shrines of the goddess Artemis whose temple was in Ephesus.

'We are losing our trade,' they said, 'because of this Christian teaching. People are no longer ordering silver statues of Artemis because these men say it is idol worship. Our trade will suffer and so will Artemis, the great goddess, if this is allowed.'

So a crowd of silversmiths rushed through the city streets to the town hall crying, 'Great is Artemis of the Ephesians', and as they ran they gathered a rabble of onlookers who joined in the shouting.

Hearing the noise and knowing the real cause of the silversmiths' shouts, Paul was anxious to be out among the crowd. But his friends persuaded him to stay at home. At last the town clerk calmed the noisy men, and as soon as the city was quiet, Paul slipped away from Ephesus.

THE HOME AT TROAS

Not far from Ephesus is the seaport town of Troas where Paul often stayed in one of the homes of the Christian community. The upper chamber of the house was reserved for the meetings of the group and there they 'broke bread' and took part in the Lord's Supper. On this occasion Paul was setting out by sea to sail down the coast on his way to Jerusalem, and while waiting for the ship to sail Paul had many meetings with the Troas Christians.

One night the upper room was crowded with people, and to cool the room on the hot night, the windows were wide open. Paul stood in the room speaking to the company, his face lit by the glimmering lights. That night Paul was more than usually lengthy in his speech and it was past midnight before he finished.

Sitting in the window to catch the evening breeze was a young man named Eutychus, a son of one of the Christian families. As Paul talked Eutychus began to doze and finally overcome by sleep he fell down from the window, in the third storey, to the ground, and was taken up for dead.

He fell asleep in the window.

Paul immediately ran down to the young man and breathed life into him again.

'Don't be alarmed,' he said to the company. 'He will live.' Then to everyone's surprise Paul returned to the upper room and went on with his address until daybreak.

Acts 16, 17, 18, 19. 28–41, 20. 7–12

25 PEOPLE IN AUTHORITY

So the tribune came and said to him, 'Tell me, are you a Roman citizen?' And he said, 'Yes.' The tribune answered, 'I bought this citizenship for a large sum.' Paul said, 'But I was born a citizen.' So those who were about to examine him withdrew from him instantly; and the tribune also was afraid, for he realized that Paul was a Roman citizen and that he had bound him.

Acts 22. 27–29.

THE MOB surged round the Temple area in Jerusalem. The narrow streets leading to the Temple were crowded with people eager to see what was happening. Few of them knew what the uproar was about except that someone had defiled the Temple area by bringing in a non-Jew.

'Men of Israel, help. This man is bringing Greeks into the Temple. He is defiling the holy place.'

That cry was enough to madden the crowd which roared out in anger: 'Kill him, kill him.'

Down through the city streets ran the news. It trickled into the house of the High Priest, into the palace of the Roman governor, and into the police station where the head of the Roman city guard was on the alert for trouble in Jerusalem. He had to be ready at all times to deal with the Jewish authorities, who were very sensitive about their customs and their traditions. As the head of the Roman guard, it was his business to keep order in the city, to prevent riots, and to see that the people of many different races visiting Jerusalem did not quarrel and fight.

So the captain of the guard at once ordered his centurions and soldiers to march towards the Temple area. In close order the men quickly got through the streets, clearing a way for themselves as they marched to the Temple gates. The noise of the mob, and the shouts of 'Kill him, kill him,' warned the captain that the mob was getting unruly. Swinging into the Temple area, he saw the crowd beating a man. His

Roman soldiers march to the Temple area to prevent a Jewish riot.

clothes were torn and the mob was pounding his head and face, but at the sight of the captain and the soldiers the beating stopped.

'What has this man done?' asked the Roman captain.

'Away with him, away with him,' was all the answer he could get. Some shouted one thing and some another, and the confusion was so great that the captain ordered the man to be chained and led to the soldiers' barracks.

Turning to the prisoner, the captain asked, 'Who are you? Are you a Greek?'

'I am Paul, a Jew, of Tarsus, a citizen of no mean city. I beg you to let me speak to the people.' Then in clear, unmistakable Hebrew, Paul spoke to the people and a great hush fell on the crowd as he told his life story. The crowd listened intently as Paul told them of his faith in Jesus of Nazareth, his conversion, and his belief that all men must be baptized and call on Jesus as the Holy One of God.

Then the uproar began again,

*'Away with him!
Kill him!'*

'Away with such a fellow! He ought not to be allowed to live,' they shouted. They waved their garments about their heads, threw dust in the air and would have beaten Paul to death except for the protection of the captain and his soldiers.

The captain then commanded his men to take Paul to the barracks away from the mob, in order to find out who this man really was and whether his story was true. He was about to have him flogged according to the Roman custom, when Paul turned to the Roman centurion and asked, 'Is it lawful for you to flog a Roman citizen who is uncondemned?'

'What?' said the captain, 'are you a Roman citizen? I bought this privilege with a large sum of money. How about you?'

'I was born a Roman citizen,' said Paul, 'and claim all the privileges and protection that I am entitled to.'

At this news the captain ordered Paul to be freed from his chains but kept in prison until the council of the Jews should meet the next day to make clear their charge against Paul.

'Brethren,' said Paul when the council met, 'I am a Jew of the Jews, but I believe in Jesus of Nazareth. I believe that he is risen from the dead. I believe in his resurrection.'

When they heard this the Jews broke into wild shrieks, and rushed towards Paul ready to tear him to pieces. But again the captain of the guard rescued him and brought him into the safety of the soldiers' barracks.

The next day the Jews began secretly to plot against Paul, and a group of forty determined men swore an oath that they would neither eat nor drink till they had killed him. But their secret plot leaked out, and Paul's nephew warned the captain of the guard of the plan to kidnap Paul and kill him.

At once the captain of the guard made his plan to send Paul out of Jerusalem down to Caesarea, the Roman headquarters, to be judged by the Roman governor. At nine o'clock at night his centurions assembled two hundred men in the barrack square for the journey to Caesarea. The road was lonely and dangerous and to make quite sure of the safety of the prisoner the captain ordered a further seventy horsemen and two hundred spearmen to go with the foot soldiers.

Paul was mounted on a horse in the midst of this small army of over four hundred men and seventy horses, and the cavalcade marched in close formation. The Roman captain in Jerusalem was taking no chance on the safety of his prisoner.

'This man,' he wrote to the Roman governor Felix, 'was about to be killed by the Jews, but I rescued him on learning that he was a Roman citizen. I found nothing deserving death or imprisonment. I now send him to you so that his accusers may state before you what they have against him.'

APPEAL TO CAESAR

On their captain's instructions, the centurions led the cavalcade through the night as far as Antipatris—about halfway to Caesarea. There they sent back the foot soldiers to Jerusalem and went on with the horsemen and Paul to Caesarea to the governor Felix.

'I must wait until your accusers come from Jerusalem,' said Felix to Paul. 'My wife Drusilla, who is a Jewess, also wants to hear what you have to say. We are interested in this Jesus of Nazareth story.' He gave orders that while Paul was kept in prison he should also have freedom to see his friends, and freedom to speak to them, and freedom to write. For two years Paul was kept in Caesarea, and often had talks with Felix and

Four hundred soldiers escorted Paul to the Roman governor.

his wife, until there came a new governor, Festus, who took up Paul's case and ordered Paul to be brought before him.

'Do you wish to be tried by me before the Jews in Jerusalem on these charges?' he asked Paul.

'I stand before the judgment of Caesar. If I have done anything worthy of death I do not wish to escape death. I appeal to Caesar.'

'Then to Caesar you shall go,' replied Festus.

The case of Paul—Roman citizen, and believer in the resurrection of Jesus of Nazareth—was now before the highest authority of the Roman Empire. A Roman citizen had the right to ask that he should be judged by the emperor himself, and be allowed to go to Rome itself to present his case.

By his appeal to Caesar, Paul lifted the question about Jesus of Nazareth from being a petty, local squabble among the Jews in Jerusalem to the highest court of all. He dared to take his belief in Jesus as the Lord and Saviour of all men into the palace of the emperor in Rome, for he was confident that he could preach the good news of Jesus to people of authority everywhere.

So when King Herod Agrippa came down to Caesarea from Jerusalem to welcome Festus as the new Roman governor, Paul was eager to lay his case before Agrippa.

'I think myself fortunate, King Agrippa,' he said, 'that I can make my defence against all the accusations of the Jews before you, because you are familiar with all our Jewish customs and traditions. From my boyhood I have been a strict Jew, and I became convinced that those who believed in Jesus of Nazareth should be punished and I did my best to persecute them. But my eyes were opened on the road to Damascus. This Jesus of Nazareth appeared to me in a flash of light and I saw a vision of him as the Christ, the Son of God. I have not been disobedient to the heavenly vision, King Agrippa.'

'This man Paul must be mad.'

PAUL BEFORE AGRIPPA

Paul's eloquent words rang round the audience chamber in Caesarea, where the king and the governor sat surrounded by the civil and military leaders. Short in stature, hunched and bent in appearance, Paul was not particularly attractive to look at, but when he started to speak then his torrent of words compelled admiration.

Festus and Agrippa, with his sister Bernice, sat spellbound under the influence of Paul's words.

'Paul, you are mad: your great learning is turning your head,' cried Festus in a loud voice.

'Most excellent Festus,' replied Paul, 'I am not mad. I am only speaking the sober truth. King Agrippa too knows about these things. He believes in the prophets. All that I have said is common knowledge among the Jews.'

'You think to make me a Christian in a short time,' mocked Agrippa.

'Short or long,' said Paul, 'I wish that everyone in this hall might believe as I do and might become like me—except for these chains.'

Paul held up both his hands locked together in chains. Prisoner though he was, he dominated the whole assembly. All eyes were on him and his chained hands were symbols of his powerful presence, which dwarfed everyone else.

Roman governor and Jewish king were alike fascinated by this man who spoke so clearly and triumphantly to those in authority.

'This man is doing nothing wrong,' they said, 'he cannot be convicted. He cannot be put to death, or even imprisoned. He must be freed.'

'He could be freed at once' said Agrippa, 'if only he had not appealed to Caesar.'

From Caesarea Paul set out on the long sea voyage to Rome.

VOYAGE TO ROME

The ship was drifting hopelessly on the high seas, and the sailors were taking soundings, fathom by fathom, as she drifted nearer to the shore.

Driven by the south wind, the ship with Paul and other prisoners on board had been running helplessly before the face of the tempest. For days neither sun nor stars were seen to give the captain his course across the Mediterranean Sea on the way to Rome. To lighten the ship he had thrown his cargo and much of the ship's tackle overboard, but with the wind blowing him helplessly before it, the captain had given up all hope of being saved. Some of the crew were making plans to escape from the ship, and had already lowered a boat into the raging sea when Paul called to the centurion, 'Unless the men stay in the ship, we cannot be saved. My vision from God tells me that we must all stay together. Let no one attempt to escape.'

The captain in charge of the ship and the centurion in charge of the prisoners were both under the spell of this strange man they were taking across the seas to Rome. It was his courage that kept up their spirits as the mountainous waves crashed into the ship. He prophesied that no one would be drowned although the ship would run aground and they would all be thrown into the sea.

All through the night the ship tossed on the waves. Twenty fathoms was sounded, and then fifteen, as the rocks came nearer. Out went four anchors from the stern of the ship in a last effort to hold the ship steady—and they all prayed for the daylight to come. When at last the dawn came the captain hoisted his foresail and drove the ship on to the beach of the unknown island. There the bow of the ship stuck while the stern was battered to pieces by the surf.

'Kill the prisoners lest they escape,' cried the soldiers, but the centurion resisted his men's demand. To kill the prisoners meant killing this man Paul, and that he would

The ship ran helplessly before the storm.

147

'He's bound to die from the snake bite.'

never do. So everyone leaped overboard into the boiling surf, and by swimming and clutching to pieces of wood, they all came safely to the shore, and no prisoners escaped.

There on the island of Malta the shipwrecked company stayed for three months enjoying the kindness of the people.

Soon after they landed, the people realized that Paul was a very special kind of prisoner. To welcome the shipwrecked men on a cold rainy day, a fire had been lit on the beach, and Paul gathered sticks and put them on the fire. As the heat warmed the sticks, a snake uncurled itself out of the bundle and fastened itself on to Paul's hand.

'This prisoner must be a murderer,' whispered the onlookers as the snake clung to Paul's arm.

'He has escaped from drowning, but he is bound to die from the snake bite.'

They waited in fear and terror expecting to see Paul's arm swell up, and to see him fall down dead. But Paul calmly shook off the snake from his arm into the fire and was unharmed.

The man of authority on the island of Malta was Publius, whose father lay ill with fever. When Paul heard of this he visited him, prayed, laid hands on him and healed him—an act which brought all the sick people of Malta to Paul in order to be healed. From being just a prisoner on his way to be tried, Paul became to the people of Malta a miracle worker and a prophet. When he left, after three months on the island, they loaded him with many gifts.

Paul came at last to the land of Italy and to the city of Rome, the seat of final authority in the Roman Empire. For nearly thirty years he had been preaching the good news of Jesus and the Resurrection. His restless energy had taken him from Jerusalem to the chief cities of Asia Minor and of Greece. He had travelled the Roman roads and enjoyed the privileges of being a Roman citizen, and now he had come to Rome itself to claim a fair trial at the hands of the emperor and to preach the Gospel in Caesar's city.

A little group of Roman Christians went out to meet him and to bring him into the city, where he was allowed to live in his own hired house with just one soldier responsible for his safety.

Within three days Paul met some of the leading Jews of the city and once more recounted his life story. Once more he told the Jews that, beginning from the law of Moses, the coming of Jesus Christ had been foretold. He held up his left hand which had a prisoner's chain, a mark of his devotion to Jesus and to his own Jewish people.

'It is for the hope of Israel,' he said, 'that I am bound with this chain.'

So for two years Paul of Tarsus preached Jesus in the city of Rome, receiving all who came to see him in his house. A preacher, but also a prisoner, Paul never ceased to be a witness to the truth that God had given him. By his words but also by his life he continued faithful to his heavenly vision.

Acts 21. 27–36, 22–28

26 PEOPLE OF THE CHURCHES

For consider your call, brethren; not many of you were wise according to worldly standards, not many were powerful, not many were of noble birth; but God chose what is foolish in the world to shame the wise, God chose what is weak in the world to shame the strong, God chose what is low and despised in the world, even things that are not, to bring to nothing things that are.

I Corinthians 1. 26–28.

The news ran through the back streets of Corinth.

'THEY'VE COME from Ephesus, and have brought a letter from Paul. Come to the reading of the letter tonight.'

So ran the news among the Christians in the city of Corinth. Through the back streets, in the shops, along the harbour front and in the homes of the people, the news of a letter from Paul excited everybody. They were all glad too to see Stephanas, and Fortunatus, and Achaicus again, who had been across the sea to visit Paul in Ephesus.

That night the letter-scroll was opened, and the three messengers who had brought it to Corinth read aloud the long letter which Paul had written in Ephesus to 'the Church of God' in Corinth.

Stephanas, Fortunatus and Achaicus knew how long it had taken Paul to compose the letter, for he had put all his heart into it. They watched the faces of their fellow-Christians in Corinth as the words were read out. None of them in the room were important or learned people. But some of them thought they were wiser than the rest, and they often quarrelled among themselves.

'I appeal to you,' wrote Paul, 'that you all agree, and that you be united and of the same mind.' The three men knew how much Paul wished that Christians in Corinth would agree to live in friendship and love.

Some of them said they were followers of Apollos, who had also preached in Corinth, while others said they followed Paul. 'Is Christ divided?' wrote Paul, 'Was Paul crucified for you?' The words of the letter were a sharp reminder to the Corinthians that they all belonged to Christ.

Only part of the letter was read that night, for it was too long to read at one hearing. The meeting room emptied and the little groups of Christians went off to their homes. Some of them were traders in cloth, some worked in the harbour among the ships, others made dyes, and some were potters and armour makers. Like most people in Corinth, they were keen to make money, which made them greedy and forgetful of their love towards each other. They liked luxury, and easy living, and the things that money could buy.

They even brought their worldly habits into the worship of the church, quarrelling among themselves about who should be leader, who should speak at the church meeting, and they behaved badly at the Lord's Supper. They turned the sacred memorial meal into an occasion of eating and drinking and forgot its meaning altogether.

All this Paul referred to in his letter, and as they listened to the reading of it, the Corinthian Christians knew that Paul had put his finger on much that was wrong in their life. Paul called them 'the body of Christ' and he described how the different parts of the human body worked together—the head, the hand, the foot, the eye—for the good of the whole body. That was how the 'body of Christ' should work, he said.

He pointed out that the different members of the church had different functions—apostles, prophets, teachers, healers, helpers and organizers. Not every person in the church had the same gifts but they could all work together in love for the common good.

The secret of the Christian way, was the practice of love, for without that everything else was useless. 'Love is patient and kind,' he wrote, 'it is not arrogant or rude, and does not insist on its own way. Love bears all things, believes all things, hopes all things, endures all things—it never ends.'

Crowded into their meeting room, the Corinthian Christians heard Paul's letter to the end. They noted especially his reference to taking up a collection on the first day of every week, and also the news that he was sending Timothy to visit them and was soon coming himself. Everyone was glad that he mentioned Stephanas, Fortunatus and Achaicus who had gone to be with him, and the reference to their old friends Aquila and Priscilla, who once lived in Corinth, showed how much Paul was in touch with Corinthian affairs. It was a good letter. There was something in it for everyone in the church.

The meeting room was packed.

THE SLAVE WHO CAME BACK

It was morning prayer-time in the home of Philemon in Colossae and the household was gathered to worship following the Christian custom. There was Philemon, the head of the household—a Roman citizen and a respected man in the city of Colossae. With him was his wife, Apphia, and his son, Archippus, his servants and his slaves. Every day they met together as 'the church in the house' to worship God, and to remember that in the midst of the city of Colossae they were followers of Jesus Christ.

But that morning Philemon's face showed that something very special had happened, and everyone in the 'church' was eager to know what it was. His face was shining with excitement.

'Onesimus is coming back,' he exclaimed. 'I have here a letter from Paul telling me all about it. Tychicus has brought the letter all the way from Rome.'

151

Onesimus coming back! The slave who ran away!

The slaves in the 'church' in Philemon's house looked anxiously at Philemon to hear what he would say about Onesimus. A runaway slave could be harshly treated by his master, and Onesimus had been away a long time. He had even gone as far as Rome. Now he was coming back, but would he be welcomed back or would he be severely punished? These thoughts flashed through the minds of Philemon's slaves as they watched their master unroll the scroll of the letter which Paul had written to him.

'I appeal to you for my child, Onesimus,' read Philemon, 'whose father I have become in my imprisonment. I am sending him back to you, sending my very heart. I would have been glad to keep him with me, but he is your property and everything must be done with your consent.'

Philemon reads the letter from Paul.

Line by line Philemon read out Paul's words. It seemed strange to the listening group that they were hearing about someone they knew, who had been part of their life in Colossae.

'Take Onesimus back—no longer as a slave but more than a slave. Take him back as a fellow-worker for Christ. If he owes you anything, I will pay it.' As Philemon read the words they sounded like a command from Paul. It seemed like an order from Paul, and Philemon's slaves wondered how their master would take it.

Philemon read on.

'Confident in your obedience, I know that you will do even more than I say. For love's sake, I appeal to you for my child, Onesimus.'

By the time Philemon had finished reading the letter, the little 'church' in the house knew that Onesimus would be welcomed back into Philemon's family for 'love's sake'. This slave who had run away would not be punished but would be received as a brother in Christ and a partner in Christ's service. Paul was so confident that Philemon would be loving towards Onesimus that he asked him to get a guest room ready as he was planning to visit the Christians in Colossae.

Then at the end of the letter came the names of those friends who were known to Philemon and his family. There was Epaphras who had preached to them in Colossae, Mark who travelled with Paul, Aristarchus who kept Paul company in prison, and Luke, his doctor and close friend.

PRACTICAL LETTERS TO PRACTICAL PEOPLE

As the little 'church in the house' in Colossae heard Philemon read the letter from Paul in Rome their hearts went out to the lonely man far away in his Roman prison who had written so personally and lovingly to Philemon.

From his Roman prison he also wrote a much longer letter to the Christians in Colossae warning them to beware of false teaching, and of philosophers who thought they had truths more wonderful than the Gospel of Christ. 'True wisdom,' Paul wrote 'does not come from man but from God.' 'True holiness,' he wrote, 'comes from putting Christ at the centre of life, and stripping off everything that is not in keeping with Christ.'

As they read Paul's letter, the Christians in Colossae felt themselves drawn into the warm, friendly circle of the writer. They were part of his parish. They thought of him as their apostle. 'Although I am absent in body,' he wrote, 'I am with you in spirit, and am always glad to hear of your good order and the firmness of your faith in Christ.'

Although far away in Rome, Paul seemed very near to the people in all the churches. He was straightforward in his letters and was not afraid to tell them where they were wrong. He was practical in his advice too. 'Children, obey your parents; fathers, do not provoke your children; slaves, obey your masters,' he said. 'Whatever you have to do, work heartily at it. Remember that you are always serving Christ.'

Paul knew that these little groups of Christians scattered about Asia Minor and in Greece were always in danger of forgetting that they were followers of Jesus of Nazareth. Many of them frequently slipped back into their old way of life, finding it more attractive than the way of Jesus. Again and again he suggested methods by which they could keep up their loyalty to Jesus, and in writing to the Christians in Philippi he put it this way:

'Whatever is true, whatever is honourable, whatever is just, think about it,' he said. Add to that 'whatever is lovely, whatever is gracious, whatever is pure and excellent.' Paul was sure that if the people in his parish of churches could keep their minds on what he called 'the things of good report' then they would be good followers of Jesus.

CHAINED—BUT FREE

Luke makes notes for his history.

For two years Paul lived in his 'free prison' in Rome, awaiting his trial by the emperor Nero. There in the prison, often chained to the floor, but frequently released so that he could walk about and write his letters, Paul prayed and planned for the welfare of his 'churches'. He was not worried about his own life. He knew that he would be condemned to death and would die for his faith. What he cared for was that these little companies of Christians might live and that the way of Jesus might flourish.

So he organized his flow of contacts. He sent out his messengers Mark and Tychicus, Epaphroditus and Timothy, with a stream of news and letters. Luke was with him constantly, taking notes and writing his history of the Acts of the Apostles. There was no time to lose. Death when it came would come swiftly and without mercy, and Paul was unafraid of it.

In a letter to Timothy, he showed how fearless he was of the future.

'I am already on the point of being sacrificed,' he wrote to Timothy, 'the time of my departure has come. I have fought the good fight, I have finished the race. I have kept the faith.' He asked Timothy to come to him soon and to bring with him the old coat he had left behind at Troas and also the books and the parchments. Paul remembered all the small details among all the great happenings of his life.

The arm of the Roman law gradually closed round him, and there came the day when, in his clanking chains he was condemned to death.

Rome won its battle with Paul. But the warfare went on. All through the churches, faithful and brave men and women remained loyal to the 'good news' Paul had preached. They too risked their lives, and many of them like the apostle sacrificed them for the Gospel of Jesus.

I Corinthians 1–16; Philemon; Colossians; 2 Timothy

27 PEOPLE OF THE NEW WORLD

> And I heard a great voice from the throne saying, 'Behold, the dwelling of God is with men. He will dwell with them, and they shall be his people, and God himself will be with them; he will wipe away every tear from their eyes, and death shall be no more. . . for the former things have passed away.' *Revelation 21. 3–4.*

FROM THE rugged heights of the mountains of Patmos, John looked out across the long, blue distances of the Aegean Sea. The slopes of the mountains went down to the sea-shore, with deep ravines separating the mountain ridges. On clear days it was possible to see the mainland of Asia thirty miles away, but with the eyes of an old man John did not strain to catch the far distant coastline. His eyes were on the bold peaks of Patmos, often enveloped in mist through which the sun would break in golden gleams. Patmos was his island world where God spoke to him. Through the sun, the mountains, and sea of Patmos, John saw his visions of the new heaven and the new earth.

For years John had been living on Patmos, banished there by the Roman authorities in the hope that Christianity might fade away as its leaders grew old and died. It was now nearly a hundred years since the teachings of Jesus of Nazareth began to spread through the Roman Empire and nothing the authorities did seemed to stop people believing in Jesus.

John on Patmos sees his visions of God and man.

In every Roman city there was a group of Christians. Even in the palace of the emperor himself and in the legions of the Roman armies there were Christian believers. They met secretly in homes and in the underground catacombs of the great cities, and when they were brought to trial for conducting secret ceremonies, their dignity and sincerity impressed the judges. Christians refused to burn incense to the pagan gods of Rome and for this a great persecution was now sweeping through the Roman Empire, and in Rome itself the spectacle of Christians thrown to the lions became a public entertainment. Even then, these Christians faced death with courage and fortitude.

As he looked out over the glistening sea, John meditated on the hardship and the perils of his fellow-Christians. Exiled from them, there was little he could do to help them in their persecution, except to pray for them, to write to them, and encourage them.

It was then that the voice of God spoke to him among the mountains of Patmos where the glory of the great heights and the wonder of God's creation lifted up his heart.

John sees the vast multitude of the world's peoples praising God for ever and ever.

'Write what you see in a book,' cried the voice, 'and send it to the churches of Asia. Send a message of hope and confidence to the people in the churches, as they face the onslaught of the Roman Empire. Send to Smyrna, to Pergamum, to Thyatira, to Sardis, to Philadelphia, to Laodicea, to Ephesus'. This meant all the world!

As John listened, his eyes were opened to the glory of God round him. He saw standing near him a man clothed with a long robe and with a golden girdle round his breast. His hair was as white as wool, and his eyes burned with a flame of fire. His voice sounded like the rush of great waters and his face shone as the sun. John fell on his knees frightened and trembling.

'Fear not,' said the man, 'I am the first and last of creation. I am the beginning and the end. I am alive for evermore. I have the keys of life and death. Write to the churches of Asia and tell them that out of their present troubles shall come the new world, and out of their present sadness shall come hope and rejoicing.'

As John listened to the voice, he knew that God was telling him what to say to the churches and to the Christians in the cities of Asia. There was a particular message for each of these seven churches.

Ephesus was commended for its endurance and patience—but warned not to give up its early zeal for Christ; *Smyrna* was urged to be ready for the persecution coming on it and not to be a quarrelsome church; *Pergamum* was challenged to repent of its

evil ways and to hear what the Spirit of God was saying; *Thyatira* was reminded to hold fast the truth in Christ and not to sacrifice to idols; *Sardis* was complimented on the honour and purity of a few of its people, but many were still imperfect; *Philadelphia* was thanked for its faithfulness although they were so few in numbers; and *Laodicea* was warned not to be lukewarm for God but to be active for God and not to be too trusting in worldly riches.

From the cities of the earth, John's vision moved to the gates of heaven. He saw there the throne of God surrounded by the thrones of the elders, with all living creatures giving worship and honour to God. As in the beginning of creation, so now at the end of time, God was present with his people, and all the tribes of Israel were there in God's presence.

THE VISION OF WONDER

But the greatest vision of all was the sight of a vast multitude which no one could number of all people, all countries and all languages, singing their praises to God in heaven. In the midst of them were groups of people dressed in white robes—men and women who had come through persecution and imprisonment, hunger and thirst, and death itself and were now living in God's presence.

As John watched this majestic scene, one of the elders came to him and said, 'These are they who have come out of the great tribulation. They shall hunger no more, neither thirst any more; the sun shall not strike them, nor any scorching heat, and God shall wipe away every tear from their eyes.'

So John wrote to his fellow-Christians and directed their hopes to the future glories which God was preparing for them. 'This world would pass away,' he said. 'Jesus would come again among them in power and great glory. Empires might fall away, and emperors would die but Christ's kingdom would be an everlasting kingdom, and Christ would reign for ever and ever.'

From the heights of Patmos, John looked into the new world and wrote of the glories that God was preparing for his faithful people. He saw the new Jerusalem, the holy city of God, coming down out of heaven. It had twelve gates, and the city walls were marked with the names of the twelve apostles. Gold, jasper, crystal and pearls decorated it, and the city had no need of sun or moon for the glory of God filled it.

THE CITY OF GOD

John's vision of the city of God saw no temple in it, for the presence of God was sufficient for all worshippers. The people of the new world would walk by the light of the glory of God and would bring all their gifts into the city of God, and all nations and all kings would come into it.

Nothing unclean and nothing false would enter the city, through which the river of life flowed in a refreshing stream, watering all growing and living things. On its bank was the tree of life, sending out leaves for the healing of the nations. Darkness would disappear. Night would be no more, and the forehead of every person in the new world would carry the name of God.

So ran the splendid and spacious vision of the new world which John presented to the Christian people of his time. The world was soon coming to an end, they believed, and the reign of Christ would begin. All the misery and suffering they were undergoing would disappear in the glory that Christ would display. They were to see the new Jerusalem, the city of God they had hoped for, whose maker and builder was God himself.

With John's vision of the new world, the Bible brings its panorama of people to a climax. The panorama began with God and ends with God. But there is a difference. In the Book of Genesis, God is not fully seen. In the Book of Revelation, he is seen in his full glory and majesty in Jesus Christ his Son.

LIST OF NAMES and PAGE REFERENCES

Quotations from the Bible are taken from the Revised Standard Version.

Key to Pronunciation

ă	act, bat	ou	out, loud
ā	able, cape	p	page, stop
â	air, dare	r	read, cry
ä	art, calm	s	see, miss
b	back, rub	sh	shoe, push
ch	chief, beach	t	ten, bit
d	do, bed	th	thin, path
ĕ	ebb, set	th	that, other
ē	equal, bee	ŭ	up, love
f	fit, puff	ū	use, cute
g	give, beg	û	urge, burn
h	hit, hear	v	voice, live
ĭ	if, big	w	west, away
ī	ice, bite	y	yes, young
j′	just, edge	z	zeal, lazy, those
k	kept, make	zh	vision, measure
l	low, all		
m	my, him	ə	occurs only in un-
n	now, on		accented syllables
ng	sing, England		and indicates the
ŏ	box, hot		sound of
ō	over, no		a *in* alone
ô	order, ball		e *in* system
oi	oil, joy		i *in* easily
o͝o	book, put		o *in* gallop
o͞o	ooze, rule		u *in* circus

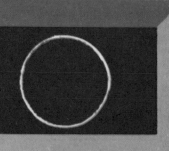